# Great Aussie Slang

# Great Aussie Slang

Compiled by Maggie Pinkney
Illustrated by Geoff Hocking

The Five Mile Press

# CONTENTS

# INTRODUCTION

Australia's rich and colourful 'slanguage' testifies to our verbal inventiveness and our irreverent approach to life. It also reflects much of our national history. Our penchant for rhyming slang (a Cockney trademark) can probably be traced back to our convict origins, while many quintessentially Aussie words and phrases date back to our pioneering past, having been coined by long-forgotten shearers, drovers, squatters and swaggies.

Our traditional songs and classic Australian poems have probably done more than anything else to keep alive much of this nineteenth-century outback slang. And for this reason, several old folksongs and verses (by such greats as 'Banjo' Paterson, Henry Lawson and C.J. Dennis) have been scattered throughout this dictionary.

Many of our more outrageous expressions gained international attention in the late 1960s through Barry McKenzie, the jutting-jawed, beer-swilling comic-strip creation of Barry Humphries (drawn by Nicholas Garland) that appeared in *Private Eye* magazine. The inimitable Aussie argot was later further popularised in the films *The Adventures of Barry McKenzie* (1972) and *Barry McKenzie Holds His Own* (1974). The typical McKenzie turn of phrase is inevitably 'a bit on the crudish side', to quote Bazza McKenzie himself, and is mostly concerned with the imbibing of alcohol, bodily functions and sexual activity.

In this age of electronic media, when our homes are daily deluged with American and British dramas and sitcoms, it is more important than ever to keep our own colourful language alive. After all, slang has been called poetry of the people, and it seems we are a bloody poetic lot!

*Maggie Pinkney*

*act the angora/act the goat*
to behave foolishly.

*after darks*
sharks (rhyming slang).

*aggro*
aggressive.

*Albany Doctor*
refreshing cool breeze in southern Western
Australia.

*all alone like a country dunny*
abandoned, lonely, alone.

*all behind in Melbourne*
pertaining to a large posterior (Western
Australian expression).

*all froth and no beer*
  silly; superficial.

*all laired up*
  dressed in your best clothes; flashily dressed.

*all over the place like a mad woman's breakfast*
  in a state of chaos.

*all piss and wind*
  boastful.

*all wool and a yard wide*
  totally trustworthy; authentic.

*alley up*
  to pay back (a debt).

*alligator*
  horse.

AMEN!

*amber fluid*
  beer.

*amen snorter*
  clergyman.

*ankle-biter*
  toddler.

*any plum?/any plum pud?*
  any good? (rhyming slang).

*Apple Isle*
  Tasmania.

*apples*
  okay, all right,
  e.g. She'll be apples.

*argue the toss*
  to dispute a decision.

*around the twist*
  insane.

*arse around*
  to fool around.

*arse off*
  to depart.

*arsed out*
  fired, dismissed.

*arse-licker*
  sycophant.

*arse up*
  to make a mess of things.

*arse-up*
  mix-up, foul-up.

*arsehole*
  despicable person,
  e.g. He's a real arsehole.

*arseholes!*
  exclamation meaning 'nonsense!'

*arvo*
  afternoon.

*as long as his/her arse
points to the ground*
  indefinitely.

*as much chance as pushing shit uphill with a
rubber fork*
  no chance at all.

*Aussie battler*
  the ordinary Australian trying to make ends
  meet.

*Aussie salute*
    the flapping away of ever-present flies from
    one's face.

*Australian as a meat pie*
    typically or authentically Australian.

*autumn leaf*
    jockey who continually falls.

*'ave a go, ya mug!*
    cricket fans' cry (to a slow batsman).

*away with the pixies/birdies*
    in another world, day-dreaming, intoxicated.

*axlegrease*
    money.

'aveago'

# b

**backdoor bandit**
    derogatory term for homosexual man.

**back o' Bourke**
    remote area of Australia.

**bag of fruit**
    suit (rhyming slang).

**bagman**
    swagman, tramp.

Who are you calling baldy?

**bagman's gazette**
    mythical source of
    bush rumours.

**bald as a bandicoot**
    having no hair.

*ball and chain*
    wife (obsolete).

*balls up*
    to mess up.

*balls-up*
    a real mix-up;
    chaotic state of affairs.

*Banana-bender*
    Queenslander.

*Bananaland*
    Queensland.

*bandicoot gunyah*
    makeshift shelter.

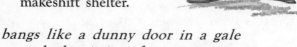

*bangs like a dunny door in a gale*
    crude description of a promiscuous woman.

*banjo*
    frying pan; shoulder of mutton.

*barbie/barby*
barbecue.

*Barcoo Buster*
westerly wind in outback Queensland.

*Barcoo rot*
festering skin disease.

*Barcoo spew*
illness accompanied by attacks of vomiting.

*bark at the lawn*
to vomit.

*barley!*
word used to call for a truce.

*barmy as a bandicoot*
insane.

*barney*
loud altercation; physical struggle.

*barrack for*
to support vocally (usually a football team).

*bastard*
most unpleasant person; affectionate appellation, e.g. What have you been up to, you old bastard?

*bastard from the bush*
rustic individual.

# The Bastard from the Bush

*As night was falling slowly*
*On city, town and bush*
*From a slum in Jones's Alley*
*Came the Captain of the Push,*
*And his whistles, loud and piercing,*
*Woke the echoes of the Rocks,*
*And a dozen ghouls came slouching*
*Round the corners of the blocks.*

*Then the Captain jerked a finger*
*At a stranger by the kerb,*
*Whom he qualified politely*
*With an adjective and verb.*
*Then he made the introduction:*
*'Here's a covey from the bush;*
*F— me blind, he wants to join us,*
*Be a member of the Push!'*
*Then the stranger made this answer*
*To the Captain of the Push:*
*'Why f— me dead, I'm Foreskin Fred,*
*The Bastard from the Bush!*
*I've been in every two-up school*
*From Darwin to the Loo;*
*I've ridden colts and brumbies;*
*What more can a bugger do?'*

'Are you game to break a window?'
Said the Captain of the Push.
'I'd knock a f—ing house down!'
Said the Bastard from the Bush.
'Would you out a man and rob him?'
Said the Captain of the Push.
'I'd knock him down and f— him!'
Said the Bastard from the Bush.

'Would you dong a bloody copper
If you caught the c— alone?
Would you stoush a swell or Pommie,
Split his garret with a stone?
Would you have a moll to keep you;
Would you swear off work for good?'
Said the Bastard:
'My colonial silver-mounted oath
I would!'
'Would you care to have a gasper?'
Said the Captain of the Push.
'I'll take the bloody packet!'
Said the Bastard from the Bush.
Then the Pushites all took council,
Saying, 'F— me, but he's game!
Let's make him our star basher;
He'll live up to his name.'

*So they took him to their hideout,*
*That Bastard from the Bush,*
*And granted him all privileges*
*Appertaining to the Push.*
*But soon they found his little ways*
*Were more than they could stand,*
*And finally their Captain*
*Addressed the members of his band:*

*'Now listen here, you buggers,*
*We've caught a f—ing Tartar.*
*At every kind of bludging,*
*That Bastard is a starter.*
*At poker and at two-up*
*He's shook our f—ing rolls;*
*He swipes our f—ing likker*
*And he robs our bloody molls!'*
*So down in Jones's Alley*
*All the members of the Push*
*Laid a dark and dirty ambush*
*For that Bastard from the Bush.*
*But against the wall of Riley's pub*
*The Bastard made a stand,*
*A nasty grin upon his dial;*
*A bike-chain in each hand.*

*They sprang upon him in a bunch,*
*But one by one they fell,*
*With crack of bone, unearthly groan,*
*And agonising yell,*
*Till the sorely battered Captain,*
*Spitting teeth and gouts of blood,*
*Held an ear all torn and bleeding*
*In a hand bedaubed with mud.*

*'You low polluted Bastard!'*
*Snarled the Captain of the Push,*
*'Get back where your sort belongs*
*— That's somewhere in the Bush.*
*And I hope heaps of misfortunes*
*May soon tumble down on you;*
*May some lousy harlot dose you*
*Till your ballocks turn sky-blue!*
*'May the itching piles torment you;*
*May corns grow on your feet!*
*May crabs as big as spiders*
*Attack your balls a treat!*
*And when you're down and outed,*
*To a hopeless bloody wreck,*
*May you slip back through your arsehole*
And break your f—ing neck!'

Anon.
(attributed in part to Henry Lawson)

*bash*
   wild party.

*bash (someone's) ear*
   to talk at length to a boring degree.

*bat the breeze*
   to talk idly.

*bathers*
   swimming costume.

*bats*
   crazy.

*Bazzaland*
   Australia.

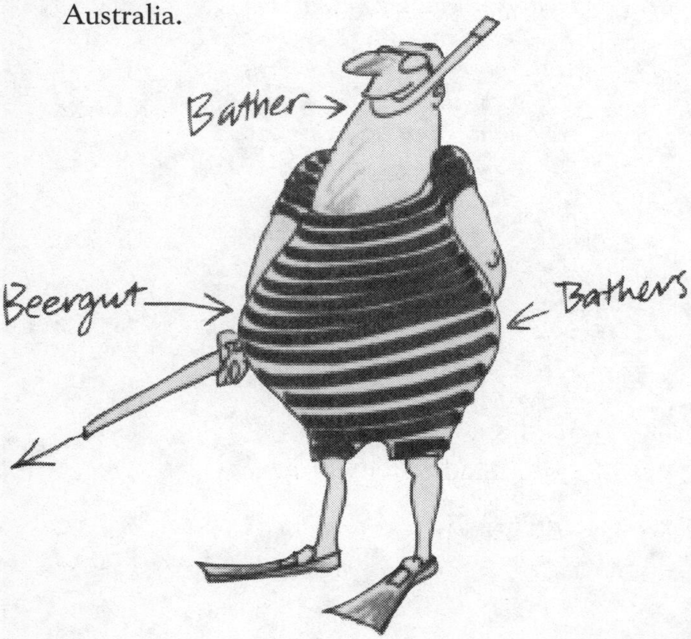

Bather→

Beergut→

←Bathers

*beat the living daylights out of*
administer violent thrashing.

*beaut*
extremely good; an expression of approval.

*beauty!*
exclamation of approval.

*Beecham's Pill*
idiot (rhyming slang: dill).

*beef*
complaint; to complain.

*been around*
to be sexually experienced.

*beer gut*
bulging stomach (of man) often associated with
heavy drinking.

*bee's dick*
smallest possible, e.g. You've got a bee's dick of
a chance of winning the lottery.

*bee's knees*
the best.

*beg yours?*
would you mind repeating that?

*belly-buster/whacker*
painful failed dive in which one's stomach hits
the water first.

*Belyando spew*
shearers' illness thought to be caused by bad cooking and conditions (obsolete).

*bend the elbow*
to drink excessively, e.g. I hear he bends the elbow a bit.

*bender*
wild drinking spree.

*bent as a scrub tick*
crazy; foolish.

*berko*
crazy; furious.

*bet like the Watsons*
to bet extravagantly.

*bet your boots on*
to be absolutely sure about a thing.

*better than a poke up the arse with a burnt stick.*
not as bad as all that; an admission that things could be worse.

*bewdy!*
expression of jubilation.

*bib in*
to interfere.

*Bible-basher*
clergyman; religious fanatic.

*biddy*
> woman, old woman (derogatory).

*big bickies*
> large sum of money.

*big-note yourself*
> attempt to inflate your importance.

*big smoke*
> the city.

*billies/billy lids*
> kids (rhyming slang).

*Billy Bluegum*
> koala bear.

*billyo*
> with great speed or gusto, e.g. The old bomb goes like billyo.

*bin*
> prison.

*binge*
> drinking spree.

*bingle*
> minor car accident.

*bite your bum!*
> shut up! get lost!

*bities*
> collective term for spiders, bull-ants, snakes, scorpions, etc.

*bitser*
mongrel.

*Black Stump*
non-existent place in remote outback, e.g. It's out somewhere this side of the Black Stump.

*black taxi*
Commonwealth government car.

*bleeder*
fellow, bloke (derogatory).

*bleeding oath!*
expression of unqualified agreement.

*blind*
very drunk.

*bloke*
fellow, man.

*blood and blister*
sister (rhyming slang).

*bloodhouse*
rough pub.

*bloody*
known as the great
Australian adjective,
because of its
frequent use.

*bloody oath!*
exclamation of agreement.

*bloody-minded*
uncooperative, stubborn.

*blow a fuse*
to lose one's temper.

*blow in the bag*
take a breathalyser test.

*blowie*
blowfly.

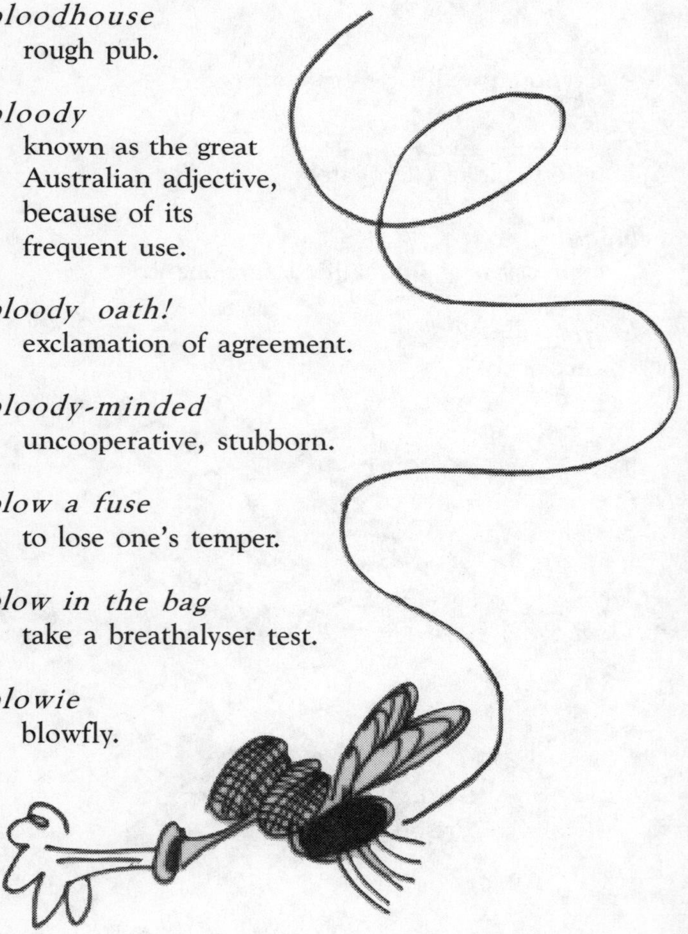

*blow-in*
  uninvited (and usually unwelcome) guest.

*blow through*
  to leave, to depart without paying rent.

*bludge*
  to cadge.

*bludger*
  one who bludges.

*blue*
  fight or argument; mistake.

*blue duck*
  disappointment; dud.

*blue-flier*
  a fast kangaroo.

*blue-nosed wowser*
  killjoy, teetotaller.

*blue-tongue*
  shearers' term for a shed-hand; unskilled worker.

*blues*
  police.

*Bluestone College*
  Pentridge Prison.

*bluey*
    summons issued by police; cattle dog; rolled up
    blanket (as used by swagmen).

*bob*
    shilling (pre-decimal equivalent of ten cents).

*bobby dazzler*
    excellence of person or thing, e.g. He's a real
    bobby-dazzler.

*Bob's your uncle*
    expression indicating everything is fine.

*bob's worth/two bob's worth*
    opinion, point of view, e.g. She put in her two
    bob's worth.

*bodgie*
    member of male subculture of the fifties, similar
    to Britain's teddyboys, identifiable by flashy
    style of dress; also means inferior, unskilled.

*bogan*
    young lout.

*boil the billy*
    to make a cup of tea.

*boiler*
    woman of a certain age
    (derogatory).

*bonkers*
    crazy.

*bonzer*
    excellent.

*boo-boo*
    error.

*booby*
    timorous,
    foolish person.

*bookie*
    bookmaker.

*boomer*
    anything
    excessively large;
    huge lie.

*boomerang*
    dishonoured cheque.

*boots and all*
wholeheartedly.

*booze artist*
heavy drinker.

*booze bus*
police vehicle used to apply random breathalyser tests to drivers.

*boozer*
heavy drinker; local pub.

*booze-up*
wild party, with plentiful supply of alcohol.

*bore the pants off (someone)*
to be excessively boring.

*bosker*
excellent.

*boss cocky*
farmer who employs labour and works himself.

*bot*
to cadge, especially cigarettes and liquor.

*botfly*
a scrounger.

*bottler*
person, thing or event of outstanding merit.

*bottom-of-the-harbour scheme*
the selling and reselling of companies (to evade tax).

*bottle-oh*
collector of empty bottles.

*bowerbird*
compulsive hoarder; petty thief.

*bowyangs*
straps buckled over trousers below the knees (obsolete).

*boys in blue*
  police.

*Bradman*
  an unbeatable opponent (in sport).

*brain bucket*
  safety helmet.

*brass monkey weather*
  very cold.

*brass razoo*
  small amount of money, usually expressed
  negatively, e.g. I haven't got a brass razoo.

*break it down!*
expression of disbelief.

*break open a coldie*
to open a beer.

*breakfast bird*
kookaburra.

*breather*
short rest.

*breeze*
easy task.

*brewer's droop*
temporary impotence caused by excessive
alcoholic intake.

*brick short of a load*
simple-minded.

*bright as a two-watt bulb*
stupid.

*bright spark*
cheerful, alert person.

*broad in the beam*
having large hips and/or bottom.

*brown nose*
to crawl to someone, to be obsequious.

*brown-noser*
  sycophant.

*brumby*
  wild horse.

*brummy*
  counterfeit; dud.

*bubbler*
  drinking fountain.

*Buckley's*
  very little chance.

*buffer*
  elderly man.

*buffin' the muffin*
  having sexual intercourse.

*bugger about*
  to mess around; to work ineffectually.

*bugger-all*
  very little; nothing.

*bugger off!*
  go away!

*buggered if I know!*
  phrase indicating one is bemused about something.

*buggerlugs*
    irreverent (but sometimes affectionate) way of
    referring to an individual, e.g. Buggerlugs here
    wants to go home.

*bugle*
    nose.

*built like the side of a house*
    pertaining to a large, overweight person.

*bull/bulldust/bullshit*
    nonsense, rubbish.

*bull artist/bulldust artist/bullshit artist*
    person who talks nonsense or exaggerates.

*bullocky*
    bullock driver.

*bull's wool*
    misleading information.

*bully for you!*
    derisive exclamation.

*bum*
    vulgar term for bottom.

*bummer*
disappointing event.

*bun in the oven*
coarse expression for being pregnant, e.g. She's got a bun in the oven.

*bung*
broken, damaged; to place carelessly.

*bung it on/bung on an act*
to act with affectation.

*bunyip aristocracy*
Australia's 'landed gentry.'

*burl*
   a try or attempt.

*burl along*
   to hurtle along.

*bush*
   rural Australia, e.g. She's gone up the bush.

*bush Baptist*
   religious crackpot.

*bush carpenter*
   unqualified carpenter, rough and ready
   tradesman.

*bush dinner*
   mutton, damper and black tea (obsolete).

*bush telegraph/bush wireless*
   the 'grapevine'.

*bushed*
   exhausted; lost.

*bushfire blonde*
   a redhead.

*bushie/bushwhacker*
   uncomplicated person from the bush.

*bushman's clock*
   a kookaburra.

*bushman's hot dinner*
   damper and mustard.

*busy as a one-armed bill-poster in a gale*
    extremely busy.

*butcher's/butcher's hook*
    a look (rhyming slang).

*butcher's canary*
    blowfly (obsolete).

*butterfly*
    a coin that fails to spin when tossed.

# C

**cabbage-patcher**
resident of Victoria.

**cack-handed**
left-handed;
clumsy.

**cackleberry**
egg.

**cactus**
dead, ruined,
spoiled.

**cake hole**
mouth.

**call 'Ralph'!**
to vomit.

*camp as a row of tents*
  of a homosexual male.

*Captain Cook*
  a look (rhyming slang).

*cark it*
  to die.

*carn!*
  come on!, e.g. Carn the Bombers!

*carpet grub*
  small child.

*carry on like a pork chop*
  to behave in a silly way; to overreact.

*carry the mail*
  to buy drinks (Western Australian expression).

*cat's hiss*
  piss (rhyming slang).

*chalkie*
  teacher.

*charge like a wounded bull*
  to set excessively high prices.

*chateau de cardboard*
  cask wine (ironic).

*cheap drunk*
  one who becomes
  intoxicated quickly.

*chew the fat*
  to chat, natter.

*chew and spew*
  a cheap cafe.

*chewie on
your boot!*
  Australian Rules
  catcall inciting the footballer going
  for a goal to miss.

*chiack*
  to tease or jeer.

*china/china plate*
    mate (rhyming slang).

*chinwag*
    a chat or gossip.

*chippie*
    carpenter.

*chock-a-block/chockers*
    full up, filled to capacity.

*choof off*
    to depart.

*chook*
    chicken, hen.

*choom*
    Englishman.

*choppers*
    teeth.

*chromo*
prostitute.

*chuck a wobbly*
to throw a tantrum.

*chuck a U-ie*
make a U-turn.

*chunder*
to vomit.

*chunderous*
nauseating.

*clackers*
teeth.

*clagged out*
exhausted.

*clagged the bag*
worn out, dead.

YOWL!

HONK!

Chucking a wobbly
& a U-ie at the sametime

*clanger*
faux pas, mistake, e.g. I dropped a real clanger.

*Clayton's*
substitute for the real thing, e.g. Clayton's caviar.

*cleanskin*
unbranded cattle or horse; unlabelled bottle of wine.

*climb the wall*
to go mad.

*clinah/cliner*
girlfriend, woman (obsolete).

*clobber*
clothes; to strike (someone).

*clucky*
desirous of having offspring. e.g. She's getting very clucky.

*clued-up*
well-informed.

*cluey*
bright, intelligent, well-informed.

*clumsy as a duck in a ploughed paddock*
very clumsy or inelegant.

*cobber*
mate, friend.

*cobbler*
  last sheep to be shorn.

*cockatoo*
  person posted to keep look-out during illegal
  activities, especially two-up games.

*cockatoo weather*
  fine by day, rain by night (obsolete).

*cockie/cocky*
  small farmer; cockatoo; cockroach.

*cocky's joy*
  golden syrup.

*coffin-nail*
  cigarette.

*cold and dark as a bushman's grave*
  very cold and gloomy.

Come in spinner!

**cold enough to freeze the balls off a brass monkey**
extremely cold.

**coldie**
can of chilled beer.

**colonial oath!**
emphatic agreement (obsolete).

**come a cropper**
to fall heavily; to have a setback.

As one cockie to another...

**come across**
(of a woman ) to agree to have sex.

**come in spinner!**
call in game of two-up.

**comic cuts**
stomach or guts (rhyming slang).

**compo**
workers' compensation.

**conchie**
conscientious objector.

**cooee!/cooey!**
greeting or call.

**cook the books**
to illegally falsify accounts or records.

**coot**
fellow, usually qualified by 'silly'.

**cop it sweet**
to be lucky.

**coppertail**
the ordinary person; a
member of the proleteriat.

**cornstalk**
person from
New South Wales.

cossie

**cossie**
swimming costume.

**cot-case**
very ill, highly intoxicated
or bed-ridden person.

*cotton on to*
  to understand; to attach oneself to another
  (possibly unwilling) person.

*cough drop*
  idiotic person.

*could eat a galah and bark sandwich/*
*could eat a goanna between two slabs*
*of bark*
  very hungry.

*could eat a horse and chase the rider*
  absolutely famished.

*could kick the arse off an emu*
  in excellent health.

*could sell boomerangs to the blacks*
very persuasive.

*couldn't fart into a bottle/couldn't fight his way out of a paper bag*
said of a hopeless, ineffectual individual.

*couldn't get a kick in a stampede*
said of a poorly performing football player.

*couldn't give a continental*
denotes lack of concern.

*couldn't give away cheese at a rats' picnic*
utterly hopeless.

*couldn't hit the side of a barn*
said of someone with poor aim.

*couldn't knock the skin off a rice pudding*
physically weak; ineffectual.

*couldn't last a round in a revolving door*
weak or irresolute.

*couldn't lie straight in bed*
of compulsive cheat, swindler, liar.

*couldn't run a chook raffle in a country pub*
lacking in organisational abilities, thoroughly
incompetent.

*couldn't run guts for a slow butcher*
very slow, stupid.

*couldn't train a choko vine over a country
dunny*
exceptionally incompetent.

*couldn't win if he started the night before*
of a slow racehorse or a hopeless individual.

*country cousin*
dozen (rhyming slang).

*couple of pies short of a grand final*
stupid.

*cow-cockie*
dairy farmer.

*crash-hot*
first-rate, extra good.

LICK !

*crawler*
sychophant.

*cripes!*
exclamation.

*croak*
to die.

*crocodile*
horse.

*crook*
    ill; no good.

*crooked on*
    angry with or about.

*crow-eater*
    South Australian
    (see also 'pie-eater').

*crumb-gatherer*
    footballer who is good at getting the loose ball
    (Australian Rules).

*crumblies*
    frail old people, elderly parents.

*cry Herb/cry Ralph*
    to vomit.

*cultural cringe*
    supposed national inferiority complex regarding
    home-grown culture.

*Cunnamulla cartwheel*
    wide-brimmed hat (obsolete).

*cuppa*
    cup of tea.

*cush*
    fair; square, e.g. We're all cush now.

*cushy*
    well paid, undemanding (of a job).

*cut*
    intoxicated.

# Stir the Wallaby Stew

Poor Daddy's got five years or more,
As everybody knows;
And now he lives in Boggo Road,
Broad arrows on his clothes.
He branded all Brown's cleanskins,
And never left a trail,
So I'll relate the family's fate,
Since Dad got put in jail.

Chorus:
So stir the wallaby stew,
Make soup with the kangaroo's tail,
I tell you things are pretty crook
Since Dad got put in jail.

Our sheep all died a month ago,
Not rot, but flaming fluke.
Our cow was boozed last Christmas Day
With my big brother Luke;
And Mother has a shearer cove
Forever within hail,
The family will have grown a bit
When Dad gets out of jail.

Our Bess got shook upon a bloke,
He's gone we don't know where.
He used to act around the sheds,
But he ain't acted square.
I've sold the buggy on my own,
The place is up for sale.
That isn't all that won't be junked
When Dad gets out of jail.

They let Dad out before his time
To give us a surprise.
He came and looked around the place,
And gently damned our eyes.
He shook hands with the shearer cove,
And said he thought things stale,
So he left him there to shepherd us,
And battled back to jail.

Anon.

*Dad 'n' Dave*
    shave (rhyming slang).

*dag*
    eccentric, scruffy person; a bit of a 'character'.

*daggy*
    someone with the attributes of a dag.

*daisy-cutter*
sports term for a ball that is thrown or kicked
very low.

*daks*
trousers.

*damper*
bushman's bread baked in hot ashes of campfire.

*dander*
anger, e.g. That really raises my dander.

*dark on*
angry about.

*Darling shower*
dust storm (obsolete).

*Darwin pyjamas*
no pyjamas, e.g. You'll have to make do with
Darwin pyjamas.

*Darwin stubby*
very large beer bottle.

*dead as mutton chops*
dead.

*dead to the world*
in a deep, possibly alcohol-induced, sleep.

*dead but won't lie down*
persistent where most would believe it futile to
go on.

*dead horse*
sauce (ryhming slang).

*dead marine*
empty beer bottle.

*deep sinker*
long glass of beer.

*deener*
shilling (pre-decimal equivalent of ten cents).

*dekko*
a look.

*dicky*
uncertain, risky.

*didn't bat an eyelid*
showed no emotion; gave no perceptible reac-
tion.

*didn't come down in the last shower*
shrewd, quick-witted.

*digger*
    gold miner; Australian or New Zealand returned
    serviceman.

*dill*
    idiot.

*dilly*
    dotty.

*dillybag*
    small bag.

*dingaling*
    silly person.

*dingbat*
    eccentric person.

*dingbats*
    *delirium tremens* (DTs).

*dingdong*
    foolish person; noisy argument.

*dingo*
    contemptible person.

*dingo's breakfast*
    no breakfast at all.

# Dinky Di

He came over to London and straight away strode,
To army headquarters in Horseferry Road,
To see all the bludgers who dodge all the strafe,
By getting soft jobs on the headquarters staff.
Dinky di, dinky di,
By getting soft jobs on the headquarters staff.

A lousy lance-corporal said, 'Pardon me, please,
You've mud on your tunic and blood on your sleeve,
You look so discraceful the people will laugh,'
Said the lousy lance-corporal on the headquarters staff.
Dinky di, dinky di,
Said the lousy lance-corporal on the headquarters staff.

The digger then shot him a murderous glance;
He said: 'We're just back from the balls-up in France,
Where bullets are flying and comforts are few,
And brave men are dying for bastards like you;
Dinky di, dinky di,
And brave men are dying for bastards like you.'

'We're shelled on the left and we're shelled on the
right,
We're bombed all the day and we're bombed all the
night,
And if something don't happen, and that pretty soon,
There'll be nobody left in the bloody platoon;
Dinky di, dinky di,
There'll be nobody left in the bloody platoon.'

This story soon got to the ears of Lord Gort,
Who gave the whole matter a great deal of thought,
He awarded the digger a VC and bars,
For giving that corporal a kick up the arse;
Dinky di, dinky di,
For giving that corporal a kick up the arse.

Now when this war's over and we're out of here,
We'll see him in Sydney town begging for beer.
He'll ask for a dina to buy a small glass,
But all he'll get is a kick up the arse.

Anon.

The great arse-kicking boot. V.C

*dink/double dink (someone)*
  to carry a passenger on one's bicycle.

*dinky di*
  really; true; honest.

*dinkum*
  genuine.

*dinkum oil*
  inside information.

*dipstick*
  crazy, contemptible
  person.

*dirty on*
  annoyed with.

*dish-licker*
  dog.

dish licker

*dishy*
  sexually attractive; glamorous.

*divvy*
  to divide up, to share.

*do a flit*
  to run away, especially from responsibility; to
  move house without paying bills.

*do a Melba*
  to continually return from retirement.

*do a moonlight flit*
   to leave at night without paying debts.

*do a nickywoop*
   to depart hastily.

*do a perish*
   to die.

*do me a favour!*
   remark indicating you want another person to
   desist from his/her comments.

*do the dirty*
   to do the wrong thing by someone.

*do your block*
   to lose your temper.

*do your dash*
   to reach one's limit.

*do your lolly/do your nana/do your nut*
   have a tantrum.

*dob on*
to tell tales, e.g. He dobbed on me to the boss.

*dobber*
informer.

*doesn't give a bugger*
couldn't care less.

*doesn't know if he's/she's Arthur or Martha*
said of someone who is stupid or in a state of confusion

*doesn't miss a trick*
of a very alert person.

*dog-box*
old-fashioned train carriage with no corridor.

*dog-stiffener/dogger*
professional dingo-hunter.

*dog's breakfast*
state of chaos.

*dog's disease*
World War II slang for malaria.

*dog's eye*
pie (rhyming slang).

*dole bludger*
someone who allegedly prefers the unemployment benefit to paid employment.

*done like a dinner*
thoroughly defeated.

*done up like a pet lizard/done up like a pox-doctor's clerk*
to be dressed up; to be ludicrously overdressed.

*dong*
to strike, punch.

*donga/donger*
the bush; the outback; the penis.

*don't come the raw prawn/don't come the uncooked crustacean*
don't try to fool me.

*don't do anything I wouldn't!*
jocular parting advice to someone going on a trip.

*don't pick your nose or your head will cave in!*
insult indicating someone is brainless.

*doobywhacker/doodackie/doodad/doodah*
term for anything of which you have forgotten the name; any small gadget or machine part.

*dooks*
hands, fists.

*Dorothy Dixer*
　　parliamentary question asked purely to give a
　　member of the same party the chance to
　　put forward the party line; a set-up question.

*dosh*
　　money.

*dosshouse*
　　cheap boarding-house.

*Down Under*
　　Australia.

*drack-sack*
　　dowdy woman.

*dragging the chain*
　　lagging behind fellow drinkers in a pub (origi-
　　nally a shearing term).

*drain the dragon/drain the lizard*
  (of a man) to urinate.

*draw the crabs*
  to attract unwelcome attention.

*drink with the flies*
  to drink alone; to be unsociable.

*drippy*
  gormless, boring.

*drive the porcelain bus*
  to vomit into the toilet.

*drives uphill with the clutch slipping*
  of someone stupid.

*drongo*
  idiot (derived from an ungainly Australian racehorse of the 1920s called Drongo, famous for coming last by a long way).

*droob*
  gormless fool.

*drop a brick/clanger*
  to make a social blunder; to impart embarrassing information, usually unintentionally.

*drop a U-ie*
  to make a sudden U-turn.

*drop off!*
  go away!

*drop your bundle*
  to be thrown by something; to give up; to give birth.

*dropkick*
  despicable or disliked person.

*drover's dog*
  disparaging term meaning anyone at all, e.g. A drover's dog could have done it.

*drown some worms*
  to go fishing.

*drunk as Chloe*
  very drunk.

*strewth!
That's dry.*

*dry as a dead dingo's donger/dry as a gum-
digger's dog/ dry as a kookaburra's khyber in
the Simpson Desert/dry as a pom's towel*
    extremely dry; desirous of alcoholic refreshment.

*dubbo*
    a country bumpkin.

*ducks and drakes*
    shakes (rhyming slang).

*ducks and geese*
    police (rhyming slang).

*duck's dinner*
    a drink of water without anything to eat.

*ducks' disease*
    having a low-slung bottom and short legs.

*duckshoving*
    pushing in (of a queue); unfair business
    practices.

*duds*
    trousers.

*duffer*
    cattle thief; mild term for foolish person
    (sometimes affectionate).

*dull as a month of Sundays*
    very boring.

*dumper*
    a wave that breaks suddenly, hurling the
    swimmer or surfer down with great force.

*dunking*
    the practice of dipping a biscuit into one's tea or
    coffee.

*dunga*
    angry.

*dunny*
    toilet, especially outside toilet.

*dunny-brush*
    'flat-top' haircut.

*dunny-diver*
  plumber.

*dusting*
  trashing, beating.

*dust-up*
  a fight or brawl.

# The Eumarella Shore

There's a happy little valley by the
    Eumarella Shore
Where I've lingered many happy hours away,
On my little free selection I have acres by
    the score
Where I unyoke the bullocks from the dray.
To my bullocks then I say, 'No matter where
    you stray,
You will never be impounded anymore,
For you're running, running, running on
    the duffer's piece of land
Free selected by the Eumarella Shore.

When the moon has climbed the mountain
    and the stars are shining bright
We will saddle up our horses and away.
And we'll yard the squatter's cattle in the
    darkness of the night,
And we'll have the calves all branded by
    the day.
Oh my pretty little calf at the squatter you
    may laugh,
For you're running, running, running on
    the duffer's piece of land
Free selected by the Eumarella Shore.

*If we find a mob of horses when the*
*    paddock rails are down*
*Though before they were never known*
*    to stray,*
*When the moon is up we'll drive them to*
*    some distant inland town,*
*And sell them into slavery far away.*
*To Jack Robertson we'll say, 'We're on a*
*    better lay,*
*And we'll never go a-farming any more,*
*For it's easier duffing cattle on that little*
*    piece of land*
*Free selected by the Eurmarella Shore.'*

Traditional

*earbasher*
   someone who talks incessantly; a bore.

*earwig*
   eavesdropper; to eavesdrop.

*easterner*
   Western Australian term for person from the
   eastern states of Australia.

*easy as pushing shit uphill with a toothpick/*
*easy as spearing an eel with a spoon*
   extremely difficult.

*egg-beater*
  helicopter.

*egg-boiler*
  bowler hat (obsolete).

*el cheapo*
  cheap and nasty; a cost-cutting individual.

*elephant's/elephant's trunk*
  drunk (rhyming slang).

HIC!

*Emma Chisit?*
how much is it? (an example of 'Strine' or
Australian pronunciation).

*emu's breakfast*
jocular expression meaning 'a drink and a good
look around'.

*Enzed*
New Zealand.

*even-stevens*
equal chance or amount.

*every bastard and his dog*
absolutely everyone.

*eyes on, hands off*
admonition that it's all right to look, but not to
touch.

*extra grouse*
really good, excellent.

*face fungus*
  beard or moustache.

*face like a chook's arse/face like a yard of tripe*
  miserable expression.

*fair cow*
  disagreeable thing or event.

*fair crack of the whip!*
  request for reasonable treatment.

*fair dinkum*
genuine, real.

*fair enough*
expression used to concede a point.

*fair go!*
exhortation for fair treatment.

*fair suck of the sauce!*
be fair!

*fairy bower*
shower (rhyming slang).

*fan-bloody-tastic!*
exclamation of jubilation.

*fang carpenter*
dentist.

*far gone*
madly in love; drunk.

*Farmer Giles*
piles, haemorrhoids (rhyming slang).

*few stubbies short of a six-pack*
lacking in intelligence.

*feed the chooks*
(of a politician) to submit to a barrage of reporters and TV cameras, and give out morsels of information.

*fit as a mallee bull/fit as a mallee trout*
   in excellent health.

*fizzer*
   failure; fiasco.

*fizzle out*
   to come to a disappointing end; to fade out.

*flake out*
   to collapse from exhaustion or intoxication.

*flash as a rat with a gold tooth*
ostentatious; tastelessly over-dressed.

*flat out like a lizard drinking/flat to the boards*
working non-stop.

*Flemington confetti*
rubbish, bulldust
(Victorian).

*flip your lid*
to become
excessively angry.

*flounder-spearer*
conductor
(of orchestra).

*floater*
    meat pie in a bowl of peas or gravy (South
    Australian).

*flog the cat*
    to indulge in self-pity.

*flophouse*
    cheap boarding house; accommodation for
    homeless men.

*flutter*
    a small bet.

*fly bog*
    jam.

*flying the Aussie flag*
    going around with your shirt tails hanging out.

*folding stuff*
    paper money.

*for crying out loud!*
    expression of annoyance.

*for fun and fancy to please old Nancy*
    facetious reply to 'Why are you doing that?'

*fossick*
    to dig for gold with a knife or pick.

*fossick around*
    to poke around; to look for something.

*fox*
    derogatory term for a member of a drinking
    party who leaves the hotel without paying for his
    round.

*Fremantle doctor*
    refreshing sea-breeze that blows into Fremantle
    and Perth after a hot spell.

*fried eggs*
    breasts.

*frilled lizard*
    man with a whisker-
    framed face.

*full as a fairy's phone book/full as a fat woman's sock/full as a goog/full as a state school/full as a tick*
  intoxicated; replete.

*full of beans*
  frisky; energetic.

*full up to pussy's bow*
  to have eaten one's fill.

*furphy*
  unfounded rumour.

*further back than Walla Walla*
  way behind schedule; last by a long way.

*galah*
someone easily duped; loudmouthed idiot.

*galah occasion*
any event that requires formal dress (gala occasion).

*game as a piss-ant*
extremely brave (particularly of someone of small stature).

*game as Ned Kelly*
daring, brave.

*gander*
a look.

*gargle*
a drink.

*garlic-muncher*
someone from central or southern Europe.

*gazunder*
chamber pot ('goes under' the bed).

*g'day*
standard Australian greeting.

*gee and tee*
gin and tonic.

*geebung*
uncultivated native-born Australian, living in remote area (obsolete).

# The Geebung Polo Club

*It was somewhere up the country, in a land of
    rock and scrub,
That they formed an institution called the
    Geebung Polo Club.
They were long and wiry natives from the
    rugged mountainside,
And the horse was never saddled that the
    Geebungs couldn't ride;
But their style of playing polo was irregular
    and rash — They had mighty little science,
    but a mighty lot of dash:
And they played on mountain ponies that
    were muscular and strong
Though their coats were quite unpolished,
    and their manes and tails were long.
And they used to train these ponies wheeling
    cattle in the scrub;
They were demons, were the members of the
    Geebung Polo Club.*

*It was somewhere down the country, in a
    city's smoky steam,
That a polo club existed, called the Cuff and
    Collar Team.
As a social institution, 'twas a marvellous
    success,
For the members were distinguished by
    exclusiveness and dress.*

They had natty little ponies that were nice,
    and smooth, and sleek,
For their cultivated owners only rode 'em
    once a week.
So they started up the country in pursuit of
    sport and fame,
For they meant to show the Geebungs how they
    ought to play the game;
And they took their valets with them — just to
    give their boots a rub
Ere they started operations at the Geebung
    Polo Club.

Now my readers can imagine how the contest
    ebbed and flowed,
When the Geebung boys got going it was time
    to clear the road;
And the game was so terrific that ere half the
    time was gone
A spectator's leg was broken — just from merely
    looking on.
For they waddied one another till the plain was
    strewn with dead,
While the scores were kept so even that they
    neither got ahead.
And the Cuff and Collar captain, when he
    tumbled off to die,
Was the last surviving player — so the game
    was called a tie.

By the old Campaspe River, where the breezes
    shake the grass,
There's a row of little gravestones that the stockmen
    never pass,
For they bear a crude inscription saying,
    'Stranger, drop a tear,
For the Cuff and Collar players and the Geebung
    boys lie here.'
And on misty moonlit evenings, while the
    dingoes howl around,
You can see their shadows flitting down that
    phantom polo ground;
You can hear the loud collisions as the flying
    players meet,
And the rattle off the mallets, and the rush of
    ponies' feet,
Till the terrified spectator rides like blazes to the
    pub — He's been haunted by the spectres of
    the Geebung Polo Club.

A.B. ('Banjo') Paterson

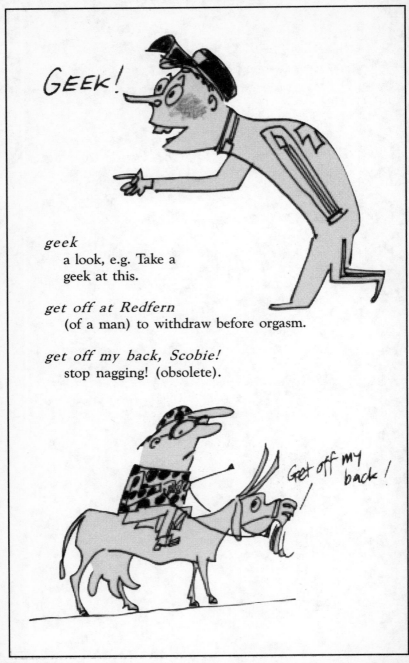

**geek**
    a look, e.g. Take a
    geek at this.

**get off at Redfern**
    (of a man) to withdraw before orgasm.

**get off my back, Scobie!**
    stop nagging! (obsolete).

*get off your bike*
    to lose your temper.

*get on your goat*
    to irritate, annoy.

*get the arse/get the axe*
    to be dismissed from job.

*get the drift*
    to comprehend.

*get the guernsey*
    to be chosen; to receive recognition.

*get your dander up*
   to become enraged.

*gibber-country*
   arid land covered with boulders or stones.

*Ginger Meggs*
   legs (rhyming slang).

*gink*
   silly person.

*gi-normous*
   huge (gigantic/enormous).

*girls' week*
   euphemism for menstrual period.

*give (someone) Bondi*
   to beat them up.

*give (something) the flick*
   to dispose of it, get rid of it.

*give you the irrits/give you the pip/give you the shits*
   to annoy or irritate.

*glutton for punishment*
   of someone who undertakes unpleasant tasks or frequently gets into unfortunate situations.

*go and take a running jump at yourself!*
   dismissive remark; insult.

*go bush*
to take to the hills; to lie low or hide oneself; to uproot oneself from the city and go to live in the country.

*go crook*
to lose one's temper.

*go dip your eye in hot cocky cack!*
abusive remark.

*go down the gurgler*
to go down the plughole, i.e. to go broke, go out of business, etc.

*go for a Burton*
to be severely reprimanded (RAAF slang).

*go for the doctor*
to use whip on horse during race; to take action of any sort.

*go lemony at*
to become angry.

*go like the clappers*
to work or move extremely fast.

*go mulga*
to take to the bush.

*go off half-cocked*
to enter an enterprise unprepared.

*go through (something) like a dose of salts*
  to consume something rapidly.

*go to buggery!*
  go away!

*go to market*
  get angry.

*go to the doctor*
  to place a large wager (on a horse).

*go troppo*
  to go berserk.

*go walkabout*
  to be missing.

*goanna*
  piano (rhyming slang).

*God-botherer*
religious maniac.

*going through life
with the porch
light on dim*
dull-witted.

*going to see a
man about a dog*
catch-phrase employed
when one does not
want to reveal where
one is going.

*going to see a star
about a twinkle/going
to visit Aunty*
euphemisms for
going to the toilet.

*gone on (someone)*
in love.

*gone to Gowings*
insane, idiotic (Sydney expression).

*good-oh*
okay; denotes satisfaction or agreement.

*good on ya!*
good for you!

*good sort*
attractive young woman.

*goog/googy-egg*
  egg.

*got space to sell between the ears*
  brainless.

*grave-jumper*
  someone who takes another's position (e.g. job, seat) with indecent haste.

*greaser*
  flatterer, sycophant.

*great Australian adjective*
  the word 'bloody', so called because of its over-use in everyday conversation.

*great Australian salute*
    motion of flapping ever-present flies away.

*Gregory Peck*
    cheque (rhyming slang).

*grey ghost*
    parking officer.

*grey nurse*
    purse (rhyming slang).

*grin and chronic*
    gin and tonic (rhyming slang).

*grizzleguts*
    habitual complainer.

*grog*
  alcoholic beverages.

*grog on*
  to imbibe alcohol, e.g. We grogged on for another two hours.

*grotty*
  dirty, unsavoury.

*ground parrot*
  small farmer.

*grouse*
  good (of a thing); to complain.

Extra grouse

*gub/gubbah*
Aboriginal term for a white (obsolete).

*gully*
a small valley.

*gullyraker*
cattle thief.

*gundabluey*
heavy downpour; rainstorm.

*gumboot*
condom.

*gummy*
shark.

*gumpuncher*
dentist.

*gunyah*
a humpy; any crudely-built cottage.

*guzzler*
aloholic.

*gyp*
to swindle.

# All for Me Grog

*Well I am a ramblin' lad, and me story it is sad,*
*If ever I get to Lachlan I should wonder,*
*For I spent all me brass in the bottom of the glass,*
*And across the western plains I must wander.*

*Chorus:*
*And it's all for me grog, me jolly, jolly grog,*
*It's all for me beer and tobacco,*
*For I spent all me tin in a shanty drinking gin,*
*Now across the western plains I must wander.*

*Well I'm stiff, stony broke and I've parted from*
    *me moke,*
*And the sky is lookin' black as flamin' thunder;*
*The shanty boss is blue 'cause I haven't got a sou,*
*That's the way they treat you when you're down*
    *and under.*

*I'm crook in the head and I haven't been to bed,*
*Since first I touched this shanty with me plunder.*
*I see centipedes and snakes, and I'm full of aches*
    *and shakes,*
*And I think it's time to push for way out yonder.*

*I'll take to the Old Man Plain, and criss-cross him*
*once again,*
*Until me eyes the track no longer see, boys;*
*And me beer and whisky brain search for sleep, but all*
*in vain,*
*And I feel as if I've had the Darling Pea, boys.*

*So it's hang yer jolly grog, yer hocussed shanty grog,*
*The beer that is loaded with tobacco;*
*Graftin' humour I am in, and I'll stick the peg right in*
*And settle down once more to some hard yakka.*

Anon.

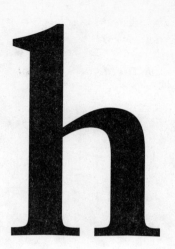

*ha-ha pigeon*
kookaburra.

*hair like a bush pig's arse*
wild, unkempt hair.

*half-pinter*
of someone small in stature.

*half your luck!*
expression indicating you feel the other person is
very fortunate.

*ham and eggs*
legs (rhyming slang).

*happy as a bastard on Father's Day*
  miserable, depressed.

*happy as a box of birds*
  in high spirits.

*happy as a boxing kangaroo in fog*
  utterly miserable.

*happy as Larry*
  very happy or pleased.

*has a death adder in his/her pocket*
  is tight-fisted.

*has a Japanese bladder*
  needs to urinate frequently (obsolete).

*has a snout on*
  harbours a grudge towards an individual.

*has got some palings off the fence/has got white-ants in the woodwork*
  is mentally disturbed.

*hasn't got a bean/hasn't got a cracker*
  is penniless; is without funds.

*hasn't got all four paws on the mouse*
  is slow-witted.

*hasn't got an earthly*
  has no chance; has no idea (about a subject).

*hatter*
  an eccentric loner; originally a miner who lives alone.

*have a slash*
  to urinate.

*have a snort*
  to have an alcoholic drink.

*have a sticky/have a stickybeak*
  to pry.

*haven't got two bob to rub together*
  is without any money.

*haven't they fed the dingoes lately?*
  jocular greeting to an unexpected guest (obsolete).

*Hawkesburies/Hawkesbury Rivers*
  the shivers (rhyming slang).

*Hay and Hell and Booligal*
expression suggesting that conditions in the
outback NSW town of Booligal are worse than
those in Hay and Hell (obsolete).

*head like a Mini with the doors open*
to have protruding ears.

*head like a robber's dog*
ugly.

*heads-and-tails school*
two-up school (obsolete).

*heart-starter*
first alcoholic drink of the day, especially before
midday.

114

# Hay and Hell and Booligal

'You come and see me, boys' he said;
'You'll find a welcome and a bed
And whisky any time you call;
Although our township hasn't got
The name of quite a lively spot —
You see, I live in Booligal.

'And people have an awful down
Upon the district and the town —
Which worse than Hell itself they call;
In fact, the saying far and wide
Along the Riverina side
Is 'Hay and Hell and Booligal'.

'No doubt it suits 'em very well
To say it's worse than Hay or Hell,
But don't you heed their talk at all;
Of course, there's heat — no one denies —
And sand and dust and stacks of flies,
And rabbits, too, at Booligal.

'But such a pleasant, quiet place,
You never see a stranger's face —
They hardly ever care to call;
The drovers mostly pass it by;
They reckon that they'd rather die
Than spend a night in Booligal.

'The big mosquitoes frighten some —
You'll lie awake to hear 'em hum —
And snakes about the township crawl;
But shearers, when they get their cheque,
They never come along and wreck
The blessed town of Booligal.

'But down in Hay the shearers come
And fill themselves with fighting rum,
And chase blue devils up the wall,
And fight the snaggers every day,
Until there is the deuce to pay —
There's none of that in Booligal.

'Of course, there isn't much to see —
The billiard table used to be
The great attraction for us all,
Until some careless, drunken curs
Got sleeping on it in their spurs,
And ruined it, in Booligal.

'Just now there is a howling drought
That pretty near has starved us out —
It never seems to rain at all;
But if there should come any rain,
You couldn't cross the black soil plain —
You'd have to stop in Booligal.'

• • • •

'We'd have to stop!' With bated breath
We pray that both in life and death
Our fate in other lines might fall:
'Oh, send us to our just reward
In Hay or Hell, but, gracious Lord,
Deliver us from Booligal!'


A.B. ('Banjo') Patterson

*hen fruit*
  eggs.

*her thighs wouldn't stop a pig in a hall.*
  pertaining to a woman with thin, widely-spaced
  legs.

*hey-diddle-diddle*
  middle; piddle (rhyming slang).

*high as a dingo's howl*
  foul-smelling.

*his/her lift doesn't go all the way to the top
storey*
  simple-minded; deranged.

*hit-and-giggle*
  sexist term for lighthearted tennis game played
  by women.

*hit the frog and toad*
  to hit the road (rhyming slang); to depart.

*hooks*
  fingers.

*hooley*
  wild party.

*hoon*
  lout; fast, reckless driver.

*hoo-ray!/hoo-roo!*
  goodbye!

*hooter*
  nose.

*horse's hoof*
  homosexual man (rhyming slang: poof).

*hottie*
  hot water bottle.

*howya goin' mate, orright?*
  popular greeting, especially between males.

*howzat?!*
    appeal for dismissal (cricket).

*hubby*
    husband.

*Hughie*
    a jocular name for the Almighty.

*humdinger*
    excellent, e.g. It's a real humdinger!

*hump a bluey*
    to carry a swag; to be a swagman.

*humpy*
    small shack.

*hungry as a black dog*
    famished.

*I hope your chooks turn into emus and kick your dunny door down!*
    Australian curse.

*I wouldn't be dead for quids!*
    a positive reply to 'Howya going?'

*I wouldn't piss on him if he was on fire*
    expression of contempt.

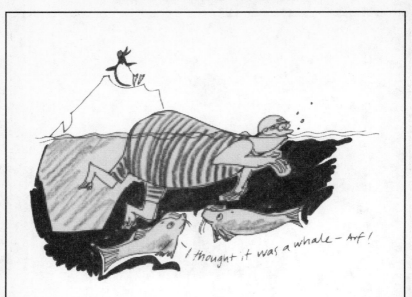

*'I thought it was a whale — Arf!'*

*iceberger*
one who swims in the sea all year round — right through winter.

*if he bought a kangaroo it wouldn't hop*
of a hopeless or unlucky person.

*Hop to it!*

*Go jnmp yourself*

*if he laughed his face would crack*
of a dour individual.

*if his brains were dynamite he couldn't blow his hat off*
of a dull-witted person.

*if it moves shoot it, if it doesn't chop it down*
said to be Australia's national creed.

*if it was raining palaces he'd be hit on the head by a dunny door/if it was raining virgins he'd be locked in the dunny with a poofter*
of an exceptionally unlucky individual.

*I'll be buggered!/I'll be a monkey's uncle!*
expressions of surprise or amazement.

*I'll knock your teeth so far down your throat you'll have to stick a toothbrush up your arse to clean them*
threat.

Just cleaning my teeth dear!

*illywhacker*
confidence trickster (obsolete).

*in a shit/shitty*
in a bad mood.

*in a tizz*
in a state of confused excitement.

*in good nick*
in good shape.

*in like Flynn*
successful.

*in the cactus*
in trouble.

*in the club/in the pudding club*
pregnant.

*in the nick*
in jail.

*in the poo*
in trouble, e.g. I'm in the poo for getting home late.

*in ya boot!*
expression of disagreement.

*inspector of city buildings*
someone looking for work (obsolete).

*intro*
introduction, e.g. Could you fix me up with an intro to that good sort?

*isn't worth a pinch of goat's shit*
no good, worthless.

*it's a freckle past a hair*
stock response if someone asks you the time, and you're not wearing a watch.

*it's moments like these you need Minties!*
expression used in embarrassing situations (from advertising slogan).

*I've seen a better head on a glass of beer*
insulting description of someone you consider ugly.

# from The Intro

*'Er name's Doreen . . . Well, spare me bloomin'*
*      days!*
*You could er knocked me down wiv arf a brick!*
*Yes, me, that kids meself I know their ways,*
*An' 'as a name for smoogin' in our click!*
*I just lines up an' tips the saucy wink.*
*But strike! The way she piled on dawg! Yer'd*
*      think*
*A bloke was givin' back-chat to the Queen . . .*
*'Er name's Doreen.*

*I seen 'er in the markit first uv all,*
*Inspectin' brums at Steeny Isaac's stall.*
*I backs me barrer in — the same ole way —*
*An' sez, 'Wot O! It's been a bonzer day.*
*'Ow is it fer a walk?' . . . Oh, 'oly wars!*
*The sorter look she gimme! Jest becors*
*I tried to chat 'er, like you'd make a start*
*Wiv any tart.*

*An' I kin take me oaf I was perlite,*
*An' never said no word that wasn't right,*
*An' never tried to maul 'er, or to do*
*A thing yer might call crook. Ter tell yer true,*
*I didn't seem to 'ave the nerve — wiv 'er.*
*I felt as if I couldn't go that fur,*
*An' start to sling off chiack like I used . . .*
*Not intrajuiced!*

Nex' time I sighted 'er in Little Bourke,
Where she was in a job, I found 'er lurk
Was pastin' labels in a pickle joint,
A game that — any'ow, that ain't the point.
Once more I tried to chat 'er in the street,
But, bli'me! Did she turn me down a treat!
The way she tossed 'er 'ead and swished 'er skirt!
O, it was dirt!

\*     \*     \*

I know a bloke 'oo knows a bloke 'oo toils
In that same pickle found-ery. ('E boils
The cabbitch storks or somethink.) Anyway,
I gives me pal the orfis fer to say
'E 'as a sister in the trade 'oo's been
Out uv a jorb, an' wants to meet Doreen;
Then we kin get an intro, if we've luck.
'E sez, 'Ribuck.'

O' course we worked the oricle, you bet!
But, 'struth, I ain't recovered from it yet!
'Twas on a Saturdee in Collins Street,
An' — quite by accident o' course — we meet.
Me pal 'e trots 'er up an' does the toff —
'E allus wus a bloke fer showin' off.
'This 'ere's Doreen,' 'e sez. 'This 'ere's the Kid.'
I dips me lid.

C.J . Dennis

*jack of*
to be tired of something.

*jackass*
kookaburra.

*jake*
all right, e.g. Everything's jake.

*jack up (about something)*
    to refuse to do something.

*jackaroo*
    worker on a cattle station.

*jam-jars*
    thick-lensed spectacles.

*Japanese safety shoes*
    thongs, i.e. backless rubber sandals with thongs
    between the big toe and other toes.

*jarrah-jerker*
Western Australian timber worker.

*jelly*
gelignite.

*Jesus wept!*
exclamation.

*jiffy*
short period of time.

*jiggered*
broken or of no use.

*jillaroo*
female jackaroo.

*Jimmies/Jimmy Britts*
shits (rhyming slang) e.g. It's enough to give you the Jimmies.

*Jimmy Dancer*
    cancer (rhyming slang).

*Jimmy Woodser*
    solitary drink or drinker.

*Joe Blake*
    snake.

*Joe Blow*
    the average bloke.

*johnny cake*
    type of damper.

*jumbuck*
    sheep (obsolete).

# Four Little Johnny-cakes

*Hurrah for the Lachlan, boys, and join me in a cheer;*
*That's the place to go to make a cheque every year.*
*With a toadskin in my pocket, that I borrowed from*
*    a friend,*
*O, isn't it nice and cosy to be camping in the bend!*

*Chorus*
*With my four little johnny-cakes all nicely cooked,*
*A nice little codfish just off the hook;*
*My little round flour bag sitting on a stump,*
*My little tea-and-sugar bag a-looking nice and plump.*

*I have a loaf of bread and some murphies that I shook,*
*Perhaps a loaf of brownie that I snavelled off the cook,*
*A nice leg of mutton, just a bit cut off the end,*
*O, isn't it nice and jolly to be whaling in the bend!*

*I have a little book and some papers for to read,*
*Plenty of matches and a good supply of weed;*
*I envy not the squatter, as at my fire I sit,*
*With a paper in my hand and my old clay a-lit.*

*And when the shearing-time comes round, I'm in*
*    my glory then;*
*I saddle up my moke and then secure a pen;*
*I canter thro' the valley, and gallop o'er the plain;*
*I shoot a turkey or stick a pig, and off to camp again.*

Traditional

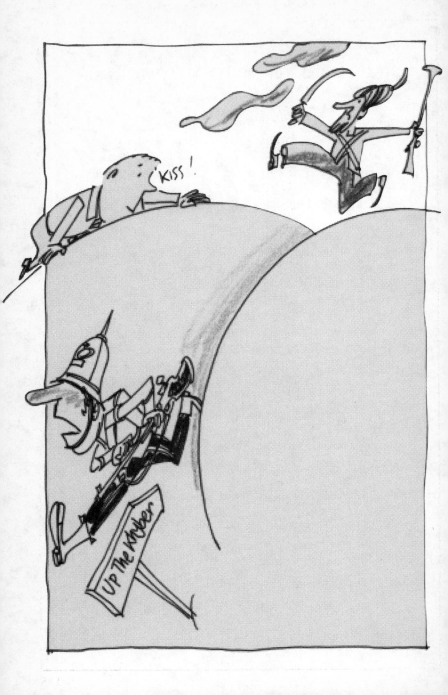

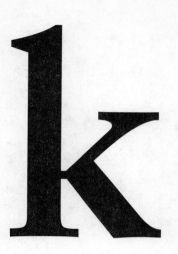

*kangaroos in the top paddock*
    crazy or insane, e.g. She's got kangaroos in the
    top paddock.

*Khyber Pass*
    arse (rhyming slang).

*kick a goal*
    to have sexual intercourse.

*kick the tin*
    to make a cash contribution.

*kiddiewink*
    child.

*king pin*
    leading figure,
    'big shot'.

*kiss my arse!*
    exclamation of disbelief.

*kite flyer*
    one who passes discredited cheques.

*Kiwi Land*
    New Zealand.

*knee-high to a
grasshopper*
    extremely short
    in stature.

Hi Shorty!

**knocker**
disparaging critic.

**knockers**
breasts.

**know a thing or two**
to be well-versed in matters, particularly of a sexual nature.

**knuckle sandwich**
a punch in the mouth.

Loose change →

*lady's waist*
gracefully shaped beer glass.

*lair*
flashily dressed man.

*lairise*
to show off.

*lamb-down*
to spend money on a drink (obsolete).

*lamb-down shop*
pub (obsolete).

*Land of the Long White Shroud*
    New Zealand.

*land shark*
    land speculator.

*larrikin*
    lout.

*Larry Dooley*
    mayhem.

*laugh at the lawn*
    to vomit.

*left-footer*
    Roman Catholic.

*lefty*
　　a punch with the left fist; one with left-wing
　　political views.

*legal eagle*
　　lawyer or solicitor.

*leg pull*
　　trick or hoax.

*lie doggo*
　　to remain hidden (possibly to avoid work).

*lights are on but there's nobody home*
　　said of a vague or stupid person.

*like a blue-arsed fly*
　　in a frantic manner.

*like a lily on a dustbin*
　　lonely, neglected.

*like a one-legged man at an arse-kicker's party*
　　out of place; ill at ease.

*like a pickpocket at a nudist camp*
　　out of place; out of one's element.

*like a possum up a gumtree*
　　supremely happy; in high spirits.

*like a shag on a rock*
　　forlorn, lonely.

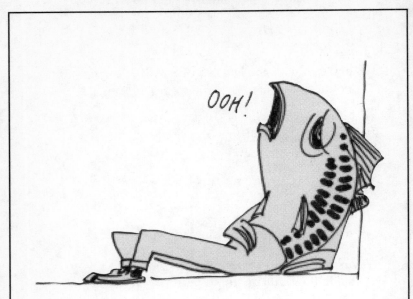

*like a stunned mullet*
  bewildered, inert.

*like a two-bob watch*
  in an erratic or crazy manner.

*like billyo*
  energetically, with great gusto.

*like the clappers*
  very fast.

*Lionel Rose*
  nose (rhyming slang).

*liquid amber*
  beer.

*liquid laugh*
  vomit.

*liquid lunch*
  lunch consisting solely of beer.

*lit up like a Manly ferry/lit up like a Christmas tree*
  intoxicated.

*little beaut/little ripper*
  person or thing of excellence.

*little Vegemites*
  children.

*lively as a blowie on a winter's day*
of lethargic person.

*living the life of Riley*
is leading a carefree, luxurious existence.

*loaded*
drunk.

*lob*
to arrive unexpectedly.

*local bike*
promiscuous woman.

*local-yokel*
well-known resident.

*lonely as a bandicoot on a burnt ridge*
very lonely.

*long paddock*
farmers' term for grassy land beside the road
(used to graze cattle during droughts).

*looks like an unmade bed*
said of a very untidily dressed individual.

*loony bin*
psychiatric institution.

*lousy/lousy as a bandicoot*
rotten, mean, wretched.

*low as shark shit/lower than a snake's belly*
  despicable.

*lunatic hat*
  a wide-brimmed hat.

*lunatic soup*
  cheap red wine.

*lyre-bird*
  a compulsive liar.

# m

*mackerel-snatcher*
  Roman Catholic.

That's the fish now for the loaves

**mad as a cut snake/mad as a gumtree full of galahs**
insane.

**maggoty**
angry; furious.

**magpie**
garrulous person; hoarder; person from South Australia.

**mainlander**
term used by Tasmanians for a person from any state other than Tasmania.

**make a proper galah of yourself**
to behave foolishly.

**make a quid**
earn a living.

**mallee root**
prostitute (rhyming slang).

**map of Tassie**
term for female pubic hair area.

I'm from the mainland

*Mark Foy*
boy (rhyming slang based on the name of a once-famous Sydney department store).

*mate*
friend; common form of address, mainly between males.

*mateship*
comradeship; the sharing of burdens.

*mates' rates*
reduced prices for friends.

*matilda*
rolled up blanket, swag.

**mean as birdshit/mean as Hungry Tyson**
very tight-fisted.

**Mick**
Roman Catholic.

**middle of nowhere**
anywhere in the outback.

**middy**
small glass of beer.

**miffed**
annoyed, offended.

**mingy**
mean, stingy.

**miserable as a bandicoot**
most unhappy.

**mockered up**
dressed up.

**moke**
horse; donkey (obsolete).

**moleskin squatter**
  working man who has scraped up enough cash to
  buy a small sheep run (obsolete).

**molly the monk**
  drunk (rhyming slang).

**molly-dooker**
  left-handed person.

**Mondayitis**
  a fictitious illness due to a reluctance to return to
  work after the weekend.

**monkey suit**
  formal dinner suit.

**mopoke**
  stupid, boring individual.

**more arse than class**
  more energy than style.

**more front than Myers**
  very cheeky or pretentious.

**more than you could poke a stick at**
   a lot.

**more-ish**
   so delicious or addictive that one wants more,
   e.g. These cashew nuts are very more-ish.

**mouth like a camel-driver's crutch/mouth
like the bottom of a cocky's cage**
   bad breath; dry mouth, especially following a
   night of heavy drinking and smoking.

**mozzie**
   mosquito.

**mug**
   one who is easily duped.

**mug lair**
   contemptuous term for a show-off.

**mug's game**
   an unpleasant or unrewarding activity.

**mulga**
   the outback.

**mulga madness**
   temporary eccentricity or insanity due to living
   alone in the outback.

**mulga wire**
   gossip, e.g. I heard it on the mulga wire.

*munga*
    tucker, food.

*murphy*
    potato (obsolete).

*Murrumbidgee jam*
    brown sugar moistened with cold tea, eaten on
    damper (obsolete).

*must have got his/her licence out of a Cornflakes
packet*
    said of incompetent driver or of any ineffectual
    person.

*mutton bird*
    Tasmanian.

*my stomach thinks me throat's cut*
    said when one is absolutely famished.

*mystery bag*
    snag, sausage (rhyming slang).

*nark*
a spoilsport.

*narked*
peeved, annoyed.

*nasty piece of work*
unpleasant individual.

*Ned Kelly*
belly (rhyming slang).

*nelly*
cheap wine (obsolete).

*nervous as a mother 'roo in a room full of pickpockets*
    very nervous.

*Never Never*
    remote Australia.

*nick off*
    to depart.

*nick*
    to steal or borrow without permission.

*nickywoop!*
    go away!

*ningnong*
    fool, idiot.

*nipper*
    small child.

# The Never-Never Land

By homestead, hut, and shearing-shed,
By railroad, coach, and track —
By lonely graves where rest our dead,
Up Country and Out Back;
To where beneath the clustered stars
The dreamy plains expand —
My home lies wide a thousand miles
In the Never-Never Land.

It lies beyond the farming-belts,
Wide wastes of scrub and plain,
A blazing desert in the drought,
A lake-land after rain;
To the skyline sweeps the waving grass,
Or whirls the scorching sand —
A phantom land, a mystic realm!
The Never-Never Land.

Where lone Mount Desolation lies,
Mounts Dreadful and Despair,
'Tis lost beneath the rainless skies
In hopeless deserts there;
It spreads nor'-west by No-Man's Land —
Where clouds are seldom seen —
To where the cattle stations lie
Three hundred miles between.

*The drovers of the Great Stock Routes*
*The strange Gulf Country know,*
*Where, travelling for the northern grass,*
*The big lean bullocks go;*
*And camped by night where plains lie wide*
*Like some old ocean's bed,*
*The stockmen in the starlight ride*
*Round fifteen hundred head.*

*And west of named and numbered days*
*The shearers walk and ride,*
*Jack Cornstalk and the Ne'er-do-well*
*And Greybeard side by side;*
*They veil their eyes from moon and stars,*
*And slumber on the sand —*
*Sad memories sleep as years go round*
*In Never-Never Land.*

*O rebels to society!*
*The Outcasts of the West —*
*O hopeless eyes that smile for me,*
*And broken hearts that jest!*
*The pluck to face a thousand miles,*
*The grit to see it through!*
*The communism perfected*
*Till man to man is True*

The Arab to the desert sand,
The Finn to fens and snow,
The 'Flax-stick' dreams of Maoriland,
While seasons come and go.
Whatever stars may glow or burn
O'er lands of East and West,
The wandering heart of man will turn
To one it loves the best.

Lest in the city I forget
True mateship, after all,
My waterbag and billy yet
Are hanging on the wall.
And I, to save my soul, again
Would tramp to sunsets grand
With sad-eyed mates across the plain
In the Never Never Land.

Henry Lawson

*nits in the network*
  crazy, insane, e.g. He's got nits in the network.

*no bull!*
  I'm not kidding!

*no buts about it*
  not a matter for dispute.

*no flies (on someone)*
  said admiringly of person, indicating quick-wittedness.

*no-hoper*
  hopeless person.

*no problem!/no worries!/no wuckers!/no wucking furries!*
  indication that a request will be fulfilled; fine!

*Noah/ Noah's ark*
  shark (rhyming slang).

*nong*
  fool, simpleton.

*nosebag*
  meal, e.g. Let's go and
  put on the nosebags.

*nose down, bum up*
  very busy.

*nosey enough to want to know the ins and outs of a chook's bum*
  excessively inquisitive; said of a prying person.

*nosh up*
  large meal.

*not a patch on*
  not nearly as good.

*not all his/her dogs are barking*
  simple-minded, stupid.

*not an earthly*
  no idea; no chance at all, e.g. she hasn't got an earthly.

*not backward in coming forward*
  brash or self-promoting.

*not bad*
  very good; excellent.

*not bad thanks — how's yourself?*
  popular reply to 'Howya goin'?'

*not for quids*
  under no circumstances, e.g. I wouldn't do it for quids.

*not much chop*
   not much good.

*not on your nellie!*
   absolutely not! under no circumstances!

*not the full quid/ not the full two-bob*
   lacking in intelligence; mentally deranged.

*not what it's cracked up to be*
   of a disappointing standard; not equal to its
   reputation.

*not worth a bumper/not worth a rat's arse*
   of little value.

*nothing between the ears*
   stupid.

*nothing out of the box*
   unexceptional; ordinary.

*nugget*
   small weedy horse.

*nuggety*
　short, thick-set.

*nut-ducker*
　person who stares at the ground to avoid
　acknowledging an acquaintance in the street.

*ocker*
    uncultured Australian man.

*off like a bride's nightie/off like a bucket of
prawns/off like a robber's dog*
    to depart quickly.

*off your kadoova*
    insane, foolish.

*off your tucker*
    having lost one's appetite; not eating.

*old chook*
 silly old woman.

*old crackers*
 elderly people, especially parents or in-laws.

*old man*
 father.

*oldies*
 parents or in-laws.

*on a good thing/on a good wicket*
 to be involved in a successful or non-stressful
 activity.

*on a sticky wicket*
 in trouble.

*on the blink*
 not working.

*on the bugle/on the nose*
foul-smelling.

*on the Murray cod*
on credit (rhyming slang: on the nod).

*on the Never Never*
on hire purchase or lay-by.

*on the outer (with someone)*
to have fallen from favour.

*on the tin roof*
something provided free of charge by the
management.

# Freedom on the Wallaby

Australia's a big country
An' Freedom's humping bluey,
An' Freedom's on the wallaby,
Oh! don't you hear 'em cooey.
She's just begun to boomerang
She'll knock the tyrants silly,
She's going to light another fire
And boil another billy.

Our fathers toiled for bitter bread
While loafers thrived beside 'em,
But food to eat and clothes to wear,
Their native land denied 'em.
An' so they left that native land
In spite of their devotion,
An' so they came, or if they stole,
Were sent across the ocean.

Then Freedom couldn't stand the glare
Of Royalty's regalia,
She left the loafers where they were
An' came out to Australia.
But now across the mighty main
The wrongs she left behind her,
She little thought to see again,
The chains have come to bind her.

Our parents toiled to make a home,
Hard grubbin' 'twas and clearin',
They wasn't troubled much with lords
When they was pioneerin'.
But now that we have made the land
A garden full of promise,
Old Greed must crook 'is dirty hand
An' come to take it from us.

So we must fly a rebel flag
As others did before us,
And we must sing a rebel song
And join in rebel chorus.
We'll make the tyrants feel the sting
O' those that they would throttle;
They needn't say the fault is ours
If blood should stain the wattle.

Henry Lawson

*on the turps*
 said of a heavy drinker.

*on the wallaby track*
 tramping in the outback (obsolete).

*on the wrong tram*
 following the wrong course of action; to be misled about a thing.

*on your Pat Malone*
 on your own (rhyming slang).

*one-armed bandit*
 poker machine operated by pulling lever.

**one-eyed trouser snake**
euphemism for penis, popularised by Bazza McKenzie, the fictional creation of Barry Humphries.

**one up against your duckhouse**
a setback.

**onka/Onkaparinga**
finger (rhyming slang: Onkaparinga, a river in South Australia).

**onkus**
unattractive; out of order.

**only fifty cards in the pack**
of someone slightly lacking in intelligence.

**only got one oar in the water**
of a daydreamer or an incompetent individual.

*only two men and a dog*
　　description of poor audience.

*onya!*
　　expression of encouragement.

*ooroo*
　　goodbye.

*open slather*
　　unrestricted opportunity.

*optic nerve*
　　perve (rhyming slang); a pervert, a lustful look.

*order of the boot*
　　dismissal from job.

*out for lunch*
　　lacking in concentration or intelligence.

*out of the box*
　　very special; exceptionally good.

*out of whack*
　　not aligned correctly.

*out to grass*
　　retired.

*out to it*
　　in drunken stupor.

*outback*
　　remote Australia.

*outlaws*
in-laws.

*over the fence*
unreasonable, unfair.

*overlander*
stockman who herds cattle over vast distances.

*Oz*
Australia.

# The Overlander

There's a trade you all know well,
It's bringing cattle over.
On every track, to the Gulf and back,
Men know the Queensland drover.

Chorus:
Pass the billy round, boys!
Don't let the pint-pot stand there!
For tonight we drink the health
Of every overlander.

I come from the northern plains
Where the girls and grass are scanty;
Where the creeks run dry or ten foot high
And it's either drought or plenty.

There are men from every land,
From Spain and France and Flanders;
They're a well mixed pack, both white and black,
The Queensland overlanders.

When we've earned a spree in town
We live like pigs in clover;
And the whole year's cheque pours down the neck
Of many a Queensland drover.

*As I pass along the roads,*
*The children raise my dander*
*Crying 'Mother dear, take in the clothes,*
*Here comes an overlander!'*

*Now I'm bound for home once more,*
*On a prad that's quite a goer;*
*I can find a job with a crawling mob*
*On the banks of the Maranoa.*

Traditional

# P

**pack of bludgers/pack of galahs**
group of people held in contempt by the speaker.

**panic merchant**
person given to panicking.

**pannikin**
small metal
drinking vessel.

**paralytic**
extremely
intoxicated.

*park a tiger on the rug*
to vomit.

*parrot mouth*
garrulous person.

*parson's nose*
fatty nose-shaped tail-end of a roast chicken.

*pass over the Great Divide*
to expire.

*pav/pavlova*
famous Australian dessert
with meringue base.

*pay through the nose*
to pay far too much.

*penguin*
nun.

*perve*
to stare lustfully.

*piece of cake*
easy task.

Thank god its friday!

*pie-eater*
resident of South Australia (see also 'crow-eater').

*piker*
one who gives up easily.

# The Pannikin Poet

There's nothing here sublime,
But just a roving rhyme,
Run off to pass the time,
With nought titanic in
The theme that it supports
And, though it treats of quarts,
It's bare of golden thoughts —
It's just a pannikin.

I think it's rather hard
That each Australia bard —
Each wan, poetic card —
With thoughts galvanic in
His fiery soul alight,
In wild aerial flight,
Will sit him down and write
About a pannikin.

He makes some new chum fare
From out his English lair
To hunt the native bear,
That curious mannikin;
And then when times get bad
That wand'ring English lad
Writes out a message sad
Upon his pannikin:

*'Oh, mother, think of me*
*Beneath the wattle tree.'*
*(For you may bet that he*
*Will drag the wattle in.)*
*'Oh, mother, here I think*
*That I shall have to sink*
*There ain't a single drink*
*The water bottle in.'*

*The dingo homeward hies,*
*The sooty crows uprise*
*And caw their fierce surprise*
*A tone Satanic in;*
*And bearded bushmen tread*
*Around the sleeper's head —*
*'See here — the bloke is dead.'*
*'Now, where's his pannikin?'*

*They read his words and weep,*
*And lay him down to sleep*
*Where wattle branches sweep*
*A style mechanic in;*
*And, reader, that's the way*
*The poets of today*
*Spin out their little lay*
*About a pannikin.*

A.B. ('Banjo') Paterson

*pipped at the post*
    narrowly beaten.

*piss in (someone's) pocket*
    to ingratiate yourself with
    a person; to flatter.

*pissed as a newt/*
*pissed as a parrot*
    very drunk.

*piss in the wind*
    to behave ineffectually.

*pisspot*
    a drunk.

*play funny-buggers/play*
*funny bunnies*
    to behave in a stupid way;
    to deceive or cheat.

*play possum*
    to feign sleep.

*play the neddies*
    to gamble on horses.

*plates of meat*
    feet (rhyming slang).

*plonk*
    alcohol, especially inferior wine.

*plum pud.*
    good.

*poets'/ poet's day*
    Friday (acronym: piss off early tomorrow's Saturday.)

*point Percy at the porcelain*
    (of a man) to urinate.

*point the bone at*
    to predict or will the failure of an enterprise.

*poison shop*
    licensed hotel.

*poke borak at/poke mullock at*
    to tease, make fun of.

*pokies*
    poker machines.

*pom/ pommie/pongo*
    English person.

*pony*
    small glass of beer.

*poof/poofter*
offensive term for a homosexual man.

*poon*
lonely, crazy inhabitant of the backblocks.

*pooned up*
dressed up in one's best clothes.

*possum*
term of endearment favoured by Dame Edna
Everage, alias Barry Humphries.

*possum guts*
coward.

*prad*
horse (obsolete).

*prang*
car crash.

*prawn*
weak, foolish person.

*preggers*
pregnant.

*proddy-dog/protty-dog*
Protestant.

*pull (someone's) leg*
to play a trick on; to tease; to joke.

*pull a swifty*
to trick someone.

*pull the other leg/pull the other one*
expression of disbelief.

*pull your head in!*
insult.

*pure merino*
first class (obsolete).

*purler*
heavy fall; indicates excellence, e.g. It was a real purler.

*purple patch*
run of good luck.

*put a cork in it!/put a sock in it!*
shut up!

*You can work this one out!*

*put on a dingo act*
to behave in a cowardly way.

*put the bite on/put the fangs in*
to ask for a loan.

*put the boot in*
    attack, especially someone who is already down.

*put the hard word on*
    to ask for a loan; to make an unwelcome sexual
    suggestion.

*put the mockers on*
    to frustrate someone's plans; to jinx someone.

*put up your dooks!*
    a challenge to a fisticuff fight.

185

*quack*
doctor.

*Quaky Isles*
New Zealand.

*quandong*
a person who lives off others.

*quick snort*
hurried drink.

*quids*
large sum of money (pre-decimal slang for pounds).

*rabbit*
to tackle around the ankles (football term).

*rabbit-killer*
blow to the back of the neck with the side of the hand.

*racecourse emu*
person who scours the racecourse grounds for discarded winning tickets.

*Rafferty's rules*
no rules at all.

*randy as a mallee bull*
sexually aroused, extremely lustful.

*rapt*
thrilled, e.g. I'm rapt about that!

*rare as rocking-horse shit*
extremely rare.

*ratbag*
eccentric person.

*rat-shit*
no good; of poor quality.

*rattle your dags!*
    get a move on!

*ratty*
    shabby; bad-tempered.

*rego*
    vehicle registration.

*rellies*
    relatives.

*Rhodes scholar*
    dollar (rhyming slang).

*ridgie-didge*
    genuine, the truth.

*ring*
    centre of operations in a two-up school.

*ringer*
    fastest shearer in the shed.

*ring-in*
a last-minute (inferior) substitute, originally applied solely to race-horses.

*roam around like a lost sheep*
to wander aimlessly.

*roar the tripe out of*
to verbally abuse.

*roo bar*
strong safety bar attached to front of vehicle.

*ropeable*
violently angry.

*rort*
wild party; scheme, deception, e.g. a tax rort.

*rotten/rotten as a chop*
intoxicated.

*rough as bags/rough as a pig's breakfast*
lacking in finesse; uncouth.

*rough end of the pineapple*
bad side of the deal.

*rough nut*
ugly person; unsophisticated person from the bush.

*rough-up*
a noisy brawl.

*rouseabout*
  odd-job man on a property.

*rubbity/rubbity dub*
  pub (rhyming slang)

*ruby-dazzler*
  excellent person or thing.

*rug-rats*
  babies, toddlers.

*rugger bugger*
  macho footballer.

*run a drum*
  to perform as tipped (of a race-horse).

*run around like a chook with its head off*
  to rush about ineffectually.

*run like a hairy goat*
  to perform badly in a race (of race-horse).

*run dead*
  to deliberately lose (of a race-horse).

*run the rabbit*
  to obtain liquor illegally, usually after hours.

*run like stink*
  to run very fast.

*run-in*
  an argument.

*run of outs*
  losing streak.

*rush your fences*
  to act without thinking.

*ryebuck*
  good, excellent.

*ryebuck shearer*
  expert shearer, a 'gun'.

# The Ryebuck Shearer

Well, I come from the south and my name is Field
And when my shears are properly steeled,
It's a hundred or more I have often peeled,
And of course I'm a ryebuck shearer.

If I don't shear a tally before I go
My shears and stones in the river I'll throw,
And I'll never open Sawbees or take another blow,
Till I prove I'm a ryebuck shearer.

There's a bloke on the board and I heard him say
That I couldn't shear a hundred sheep a day,
But one fine day, mate, I'll show him the way;
I'll prove I'm a ryebuck shearer.

You ought to see our ringer, he's nothing but a farce.
When the cobbler's coming up, he's always first to pass,
As for the shearing, he's more arse than class,
And he'll never be a ryebuck shearer.

There's a swaggie down the creek, his name is Jack,
He rolled into town with a swag on his back;
He asked us for a job, said he needed a few bob,
And he swears he's a ryebuck shearer.

Yes, I'll make a splash, and I won't say when,
I'll up off me arse and I'll into the pen.
While the ringer's shearing eight, mate, I'll be
    shearing ten,
And I'll prove I'm a ryebuck shearer.

Traditional

**S**

*same diff*
expression meaning 'more or less the same thing'.

*same here!*
expression of unqualified agreement.

*sammie*
sandwich.

*sandgroper*
West Australian.

*sandwich short of a picnic*
lacking in intelligence.

*sandy blight*
eye complaint prevalent in outback areas.

*Sandy McNab*
cab (rhyming slang).

*sanger*
sandwich.

*scab*
abusive term for non-union worker.

*schooner*
large beer glass (NSW); small beer glass (SA).

*scorcher*
swelteringly hot day.

A SCHOONER!
I'm Saved

*screaming heebie-jeebies*
intense irritation.e.g. That really gives me the
screaming heebie-jeebies.

*scumbag*
low-down, despicable individual.

*scunge*
dirty, untidy person.

*scungy*
unattractive, dirty.

*search me!*
I don't know!

*see you later*
goodbye (said regardless of whether or not the speaker intends to see the other person later on).

*seen his/her last gumtree*
on the verge of death.

*selling tickets on himself/herself*
said of conceited individual.

*septic tank*
Yank (rhyming slang).

*settler's clock*
kookaburra.

*Shaky Isles*
New Zealand.

*Shank's pony*
on foot, as against by car or other mode of transport.

*sharkbait*
   someone who swims much further out to sea
   than other swimmers.

*shearers' joy*
   Australian beer.

*she'll be apples/she'll be right*
expression said to typify the easy-going Australian attitude, particularly a few decades ago.

*sheila*
girl, woman.

*shepherd's friend*
dingo (ironic).

*shickered*
drunk.

*shindig*
noisy party; row.

*shiny-arse*
public servant.

*shiralee*
swag.

*shirty/shitty*
irritable.

*shithouse/shouse*
lavatory; of poor quality; awful.

*shivoo*
wild party.

*shonky*
unreliable, dishonest.

*shook on*
infatuated by.

*shoot through*
to leave suddenly, often to avoid paying debts or facing up to some other responsibility.

*short-arse*
a person lacking in height.

*short of numbers in the Upper House*
foolish, stupid.

*shot full of holes*
very drunk.

*shot through like a Bondi tram*
departed hastily.

*shout*
> to pay for a treat of some sort; a round of drinks,
> e.g. Next time it's my shout.

*shovel shit*
> to work in menial job.

*sickie*
> day's sick leave, often
> taken on dubious grounds,
> e.g. I think I'll take a
> sickie on Monday.

*silly as a two-bob*
*watch/silly as a wet hen*
> unreliable; dizzy, crazy.

*silly sausage*
> silly-billy, usually applied
> to small children.

*silvertail*
> a member of the upper classes; a 'swell'.

*since Cocky was an egg*
> for a long time.

*sink a few*
> to drink beer.

*sink the boot/sink the slipper*
> to kick viciously; to attack verbally.

*sinker*
> meat pie.

*snake juice*
strong alcoholic drink.

*snarler*
sausage.

*sitting on an ant's nest*
in an unfortunate situation which will only get worse.

*sitting up like Jackie*
unabashed presence in a gathering.

*skedaddle*
to leave hastily.

*skerrick*
minimal quantity.

*skew-whiff*
askew.

*skinful*
drunk, e.g. He's had a skinful.

*skinny as a sapling with the bark scraped off*
very thin.

*skip/skippy*
term for English-, Irish- or Scottish-descent Australian by Australian of ethnic origins.

*skite*
boastful person; to boast.

*skittle*
   to knock down.

*skull banker*
   tramp; swagman (obsolete).

*sky pilot*
   clergyman.

*slacker*
   lazy person.

*sly grog*
   illegal alcohol.

*smack a blue*
   to strike trouble.

*smackers/smackeroos*
   pounds or dollars.

*smashed*
   drunk.

*smoko*
   short break from work for morning or
   afternoon tea.

*snag*
   sausage; hidden problem.

*snag short of a barbie*
   lacking in intelligence.

*snagger*
    a 'learner' shearer.

*snake juice*
    very strong alcohol.

*snake's hiss*
    piss (rhyming slang).

*snakes hissed*
    pissed (rhyming slang); intoxicated.

*snakey*
    irritable.

*snowdrop*
  to steal clothes from the washing line.

*snuff it*
  to die.

*so poor he/she would lick the paint off the fence.*
  extremely poor.

*so slow he/she couldn't get a job as a speed hump*
  slow-witted, lethargic.

*so mean that when a fly lands in the sugar he shakes its feet before he kills it/so mean he wouldn't give a rat a railway pie*
  extremely tight-fisted.

*so wet you could shoot ducks off him/her*
  idiotic.

*sook*
  a cowardly individual, a 'wimp'.

*sooky*
  one with the attributes of a sook.

*soup-strainer*
  moustache.

*Southerly Buster*
  cool wind that blows up in Sydney after a hot spell.

*sparkie*
an electrician.

*sparrow's fart*
just before dawn; very early.

*speak on the big white telephone*
to vomit into the lavatory.

*speed merchant*
fast driver.

*Speewa*
legendary outback station.

*spew*
to vomit.

*spewin'!*
exclamation, usually indicating annoyance or disappointment.

*spewy*
awful; unattractive.

*spieler*
gambler, card-sharp, swindler (obsolete).

*spinebash*
to sleep or loaf.

*spinebasher*
a loafer or parasite.

*spit the dummy*
    to lose one's temper.

*spitting chips!*
    exclamation to indicate one is angry or frustrated.

*splash the boots*
    (of a male) to urinate.

*sponger*
    someone who cadges from others.

*spunk*
    sexy, good-looking person.

*spruiker*
    person who shouts to attract customers.

*squatter*
    wealthy pastoralist (derived from term for
    person who settled on Crown land without a
    permit).

*squatter's daughter*
    water (rhyming slang).

*squiz*
    a look.

*stack your drapery*
    to put your coat on the ground before a fight.

*stands out like a black crow in a bucket of
milk*
    obvious, extremely clear.

*starkers*
   naked.

*starve the lizards!*
   exclamation.

*Steak and Kidney*
   Sydney (rhyming slang).

*stick your bib in*
   to interfere.

*sticks out like a dog's balls*
   very clear, self-evident.

*stickybeak*
   inquisitive, prying person.

*stiff bickies!*
   too bad!

*still kicking*
   alive (ironic).

*stinker*
   boiling hot day.

*stinko*
   drunk.

*stir the possum*
   to create a disturbance; to raise
   controversial issues.

*stone the crows!*
   exclamation.

*stony/stony broke*
  penniless.

*stonkered*
  intoxicated.

*storm stick*
  umbrella.

*stoush*
  a fight; to punch
  or bash.

*strain the potatoes*
  (of a man) to urinate.

*strapped for cash*
  short of money.

*streak/stretch*
  nickname for tall
  thin individual.

*strewth!*
  exclamation.

*strides*
  trousers.

*strike a light!*
  exclamation.

*stringybark*
  bad whisky (obsolete).

Hey Stretch who are you calling Short arse!

*stubbie*
    short chunky bottle
    of beer.

*stuffed*
    ruined.

*stuff up*
    to mess up.

*stumer*
    defaulter (racing term).

*stumped up*
    without funds; broke.

*stunned*
    drunk.

*stuff-up*
    mix-up, blunder.

*suck*
    obnoxious person.

*suffer!*
    a taunt.

*suffer a recovery*
    recover from a hangover.

*sunbeam*
    china set out for a meal but not used, e.g. You
    can put this plate back — it's a sunbeam.

*Sunday dog*
  lazy person (obsolete).

*sundowner*
  tramp.

*sunnies*
  sunglasses.

*suss*
  suspicious (abbreviation).

*susso*
  the dole.

*swaggie/swagman*
  tramp.

*sweat on it*
  to wait apprehensively.

*sweet Fanny Adams*
  zilch, none, nothing.

*swing the gate*
  to be the fastest shearer in the shed.

*sword-swallower*
  person who eats off his/her knife.

*Sydney Harbour*
  barber (rhyming slang)

*Sydneyite*
  a resident of Sydney.

*syphon the python*
  (of a male) to urinate.

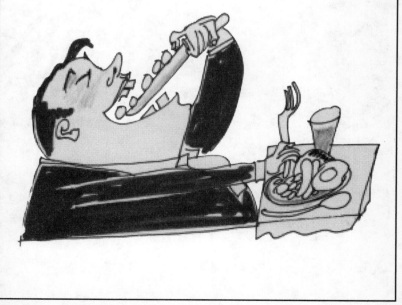

*take a piece out of*
   to tell someone off.

*take a punt*
   to take a chance.

*take the mickey out of*
   to ridicule or tease.

*tally*
   originally meaning the shearing of 100 sheep,
   now means score.

*tanked*
drunk.

*Tassie tiger*
Tasmanian.

*tatty*
shabby, inferior.

*Technicolor yawn*
to vomit.

*tee up*
to make an arrangement.

*ten-ounce sandwich*
lunch consisting solely of beer.

*that's the way the Violet Crumbles*
philosophical reflection on turn of events.

*the Don*
    Don Bradman.

*thick as a brick/thick as the dust on a public servant's out-tray*
    dull, slow-witted.

DOH!

*things are crook at Tallarook*
    catch-phrase to cover any adverse situation.

*thinks the sun shines out of his/her arse*
    to have an exaggerated regard for another person or oneself.

*thongs*
  backless rubber sandals with thong between the big toe and other toes.

*three parts gone/three sheets to the wind*
  inebriated.

*three pots short of a shout*
  stupid.

*throw your voice*
  to vomit.

*thunder box*
  outdoor lavatory.

*ticker*
  the heart.

*tickle the till*
  to rob or embezzle.

*tight as a bull's arse in fly time/tight as a fish's arse*
  extremely parsimonious.

*tin-arse/tin-bum*
term used to describe someone who always
seems to have good luck.

*tin ear*
eavesdropper.

*tinny*
can of beer.

*tinny short of a six-pack*
of lower than average intelligence.

*tip the finger*
to imbibe (alcohol).

*tired and emotional*
drunk (ironic).

*toadskin*
> five pound note (pre-decimal equivalent of ten dollars).

*toey*
> bad-tempered.

*togs*
> swimming costume.

*too right!*
> emphatic affirmative.

*Top End*
> Northern Territory.

*top-ender*
> person from the Northern Territory.

*topwire lizard*
> boundary rider.

*toss in the alley*
> to admit defeat.

*total wreck*
cheque.

*tough as fencing wire*
very tough.

*tough titty!*
too bad!

*trimmer*
excellent thing or person, usually preceded by 'a real'.

*triple-fronted brick vanilla/triple-fronted brick venereal*
ironic term for typical suburban dream-home.

*trooper*
policeman (obsolete).

*troppo*
mad, eccentric from living in the tropics.

*trots*
diarrhoea.

*trouble and strife*
    wife (rhyming slang).

*true blue*
    the real thing.

*trunks*
    swimming shorts.

*tubes*
    large cans of beer.

# Nine Miles from Gundagai

I've done my share of shearing sheep,
Of droving and all that,
And bogged a bullock-team as well,
On a Murrumbidgee flat.
I've seen the bullock stretch and strain,
And blink his bleary eye,
And the dog sit on the tucker box,
Nine miles from Gundagai.

I've been jilted, jarred, and crossed in love,
And sand-bagged in the dark,
Till if a mountain fell on me
I'd treat it as a lark.
It's when you've got your bullocks bogged
That's the time you flog and cry,
And the dog sits on the tucker box,
Nine miles from Gundagai.

We've all got our little troubles,
In life's hard, thorny way.
Some strike them in a motor car
And others in a dray.
But when your dog and bullocks strike
It ain't no apple pie,
And the dog sat on the tucker box
Nine miles from Gundagai.

But that's all past and dead and gone,
And I've sold the team for meat,
And perhaps some day where I was bogged,
There'll be an asphalt street.
The dog, ah! well he got a bait,
And thought he'd like to die,
So I buried him in the tucker box,
Nine miles from Gundagai.

Jack Moses

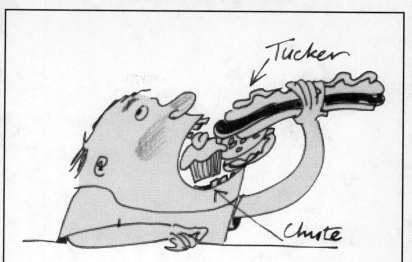

*tucker*
food.

*tucker chute*
mouth.

*tuckered out*
exhausted.

*tumble to*
to become aware of.

*turkey*
a swag (obsolete).

*turkey off*
to depart.

*turn dingo*
become an informer.

*turn it up!*
come off it! be reasonable!

*turps*
any strong drink; abbreviation of turpentine.

*twig on to*
to comprehend.

*twinkle-palace*
toilet.

*twit*
idiot.

*two and a half sheets to the wind*
drunk.

*two-bob lair*
man dressed in cheap, flashy manner.

*two men and a dog*
very few people; a poor attendance.

*two-pot screamer*

one who becomes intoxicated after a couple of drinks.

*two-up*

gambling game in which bets are made on whether two pennies come up heads or tails when tossed in the air.

*tyke*

Roman Catholic; cur, mischievous child, e.g. He's a little tyke.

*under the affluence of inkahol*
under the influence of alcohol.

*under the weather*
drunk.

*underground mutton*
rabbits.

*undies*
    underpants.

*up a gumtree*
    in trouble or confused.

*up King Street*
    bankrupt (obsolete).

*up shit creek without a paddle*
    in deep trouble.

*up the donga/up the donger*
    out in the country.

*up the duff*
    vulgar term for being pregnant.

*up the pole*
    confused, incorrect.

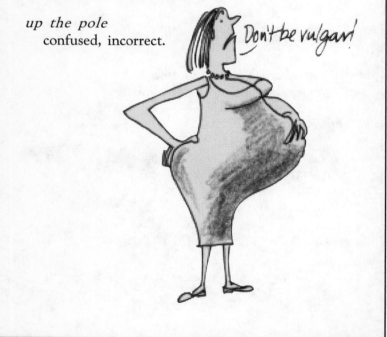

Don't be vulgar!

**up the spout**
    ruined; pregnant.

**up there Cazaly!**
    a cry of encouragement.

**useful as a flywire door on a submarine/
useful as a one-legged man in an arse-kicking contest**
    absolutely useless.

**V**

*Vandyke*
   outdoor lavatory.

*vee-dub*
   Volkswagen.

*verandah above the toyshop*
    male paunch.

*verbal diarrhoea*
    non-stop talk, garrulity.

*village bike*
promiscuous woman.

*vino*
cheap wine.

*visiting card*
any article of clothing or object readily
recognisable as belonging to a certain person.

*volcanoes*
pimples or boils.

*vulture*
driver who doubleparks, ready to claim a
desirable parking space while present occupant
is still trying to get out.

*wacker*
  crazy person.

*waffle on*
  to prattle on aimlessly.

*wake up, Australia!*
  said to daydreamer.

*walking papers*
  dismissal notice, the sack.

*walloper*
  policeman.

*wally*
    an idiot.

*Wally Grout*
    a shout (rhyming slang), e.g. Whose Wally
    Grout is it?

*waltzing matilda*
    carrying a swag.

*water the horses*
    to urinate.

*weak as a wet whistle*
    very weak or ineffectual.

*weak as cats' piss*
    very weak (of an alcoholic beverage).

*weed*
    tobacco.

*were you born in a tent?*
    said to someone who habitually leaves door ajar.

*well under*
    drunk.

*wellies*
    Wellington boots; gumboots.

*welsh on*
    to betray, inform on; to fail to honour debts.

*went through like a dose of salts/went
through without the water-bag*
    departed hastily.

*westie*
    one from the western suburbs (of Sydney or
    Melbourne).

*wet arse and no fish*
    of a fruitless errand.

*wet as water*
    very feeble or corny.

*wet enough to bog a duck*
    of extremely wet weather.

# Waltzing Matilda

*Once a jolly swagman camped by a billabong,*
*Under the shade of a coolibah tree,*
*And he sang as he watched and waited till his*
    *billy boiled,*
*'Who'll come a-waltzing Matilda with me?*
*Waltzing Matilda, waltzing Matilda,*
*Who'll come a-waltzing Matilda with me?'*
*And he sang as he watched and waited till his*
    *billy boiled,*
*'Who'll come a-waltzing Matilda with me?'*

*Down came a jumbuck to drink at that billabong;*
*Up jumped the swagman and grabbed him with glee.*
*And he sang as he shoved that jumbuck in his*
    *tucker-bag,*
*'You'll come a-waltzing Matilda with me.*
*Waltzing Matilda, waltzing Matilda,*
*You'll come a-waltzing Matilda with me.'*
*And he sang as he shoved that jumbuck in his*
    *tucker-bag,*
'You'll come a-waltzing Matilda with me!'

*Up rode a squatter, mounted on his thoroughbred;*
*Down came the troopers: one, two, three.*
*'Whose' that jolly jumbuck you've got in your*
    *tucker-bag?'*
*'You'll come a-waltzing Matilda with me.*
*Waltzing Matilda, waltzing Matilda,*
*You'll come a-waltzing Matilda with me!*
*Whose' that jolly jumbuck you've got in your*
    *tucker-bag?*

You'll come a-waltzing Matilda with me!'
*Up jumped the swagman and sprang into
    the billabong;*
'You'll never catch me alive!' said he;
*And his ghost may be heard as you pass by
    that billabong,*
'You'll come a-waltzing Matilda with me!
*Waltzing Matilda, waltzing Matilda,*
*You'll come a-waltzing Matilda with me!'*
*And his ghost may be heard as you pass by that
billabong,*
'You'll come a-waltzing Matilda with me!'

A.B. ('Banjo') Paterson

*whacko!/whacko the diddle-o!*
    jubilant exclamation.

*whaler*
    one who leads an idle, carefree existence on the
    banks of a river (obsolete).

*what are ya!*
    sarcastic exclamation used when someone says
    something foolish.

*what do you do for a crust?*
    how do you make a living?

*what do you think this is — bush week?*
    shouted by motorist to indicate disgust at an-
    other motorist's lack of driving expertise.

*what else did you get for Christmas?*
    shouted when another motorist is over-using car
    horn.

*what's the damage?*
    how much do I owe?

*what the bloody hell's crawlin' on you, mate?*
    a put-down.

*whatcha-m'-call it!/waddya-call it*
    anything at all, especially if you have forgotten its name.

*what's your beef?*
    what's your problem

*when the eagle shits*
    payday.

*when the shit hits the fan*
    when a problem or mistake comes out into the open and reaches its peak.

*where the crows fly backwards to keep the dust out of their eyes*
    any remote outstation.

FLAP! FLAP! FLAP!

*whinge*
    whine; whining complaint.

*whingeing Pom*
    dissatisfied English migrant.

*whinger*
    habitual complainer.

*white ant*
    to sabotage.

*whip the cat*
    to reproach oneself (ironic).

*whippersnapper*
    child or cheeky young person.

*whirl*
    try or go, e.g. Give it a whirl!

*whoopydoo!*
    enthusiastic exclamation, sometimes used
    sarcastically.

*whopper*
    anything enormous; a huge lie.

*who's robbing this coach?*
    said when someone else is interfering (obsolete).

*why keep a dog and bark yourself?*
    rhetorical question pointing out the futility of
    carrying out duties which you have employed
    someone else (better qualified) to perform.

*widgie*
female counterpart of 'bodgie'.

*Williamstown piers*
ears (rhyming slang).

*will get gravel rash*
said of someone acting in a sychophantic
manner.

*willies*
feeling of apprehension, e.g. Something about
him gives me the willies.

*windy enough to blow a blue dog off its
chain*
extremely windy.

*within cooee/cooey*
quite close; almost, e.g. He was within cooee of
getting elected.

*wonky*
unsteady, shaky.

*won't have a bar of*
    refuses to have any part of a thing.

*wool-classer*
    a dog that bites sheep.

*Woolloomooloo uppercut*
    kick in the groin.

*Woolloomooloo Yank*
    a World War II term for a local youth affecting
    American airs or assuming an American accent.

*Woop-Woop*
    fictitious remote area
    of Australia.

*Woop-Woop pigeon*
  kookaburra.

*would bet on two flies walking up the wall*
  of a compulsive gambler.

*would give you the Jimmies/would give you*
*the Jimmy Britts*
  would give you the shits (rhyming slang).

*would knock your socks off*
  of something amazing.

*would talk a glass eye to sleep*
  of excessively boring individual.

*wouldn't give you the time of day*
   of uncooperative, stand-offish or excessively
   mean person.

*wouldn't it rip you!/wouldn't it rot your
socks!/wouldn't it root you!*
   indicates annoyance or disgust.

*wouldn't know his arse from his elbow*
   of an idiotic person.

*wouldn't piss on you if you were on fire*
   said of an excessively mean-spirited individual.

*wouldn't shout in a shark attack*
   of an exceptionally parsimonious person; of a
   dull-witted individual.

*wouldn't touch it with a forty foot pole*
   wouldn't have anything to do with it.

*wouldn't use him/her for sharkbait*
> of an individual one holds in extremely low regard.

*wouldn't work in an iron lung*
> of an excessively lazy individual.

*wowser*
> killjoy; one who disapproves of drinking, gambling and dancing.

# y

*yabber*
to talk at
great speed;
to chatter.

*yakka*
physical
labour.

*Yank bait*
derogatory World War ll term for Australian
women hoping to attract the affections of
American servicemen.

*yellow fever*
  gold fever.

*yobbo*
  lout.

*yodel*
  to vomit.

*yoe*
  sheep, ewe (obsolete).

*yonnie*
  flat stone or pebble suitable for skimming on water.

*you beaut!/you little beauty!*
  jublilant exclamation.

*you der!*
  you idiot!

*you'd make a blowfly sick!*
  insult.

*you're not wrong!*
  term of wholehearted agreement.

*your blood's worth bottling*
  said to someone one admires, or to one who has done something excellent.

*yowie*
  mythical Australian monster.

# Click Go the Shears

Out on the board the old shearer stands,
Grasping his shears in his thin bony hands;
Fixed is his gaze on a bare-bellied yoe,
Glory if he gets her, won't he make the ringer go.

Chorus
Click go the shears, boys, click, click, click,
Wide is his blow and his hands move quick,
The ringer looks around and is beaten by a blow,
And curses the old snagger with the bare-bellied yoe.

In the middle of the floor, in his cane-bottomed chair
Is the boss of the board, with eyes everywhere;
Notes well each fleece as it comes to the screen,
Paying strict attention if it's taken off clean.

The colonial experience man, he is there, of course,
With his shiny leggin's, just got off his horse;
Casting round his eye, like a real connoisseur,
Whistling the old tune, 'I'm the Perfect Lure.'

The tar-boy is there, awaiting in demand,
With his blackened tar-pot, and his tarry hand,
Sees one old sheep with a cut upon its back,
Hears what he's waiting for, 'Tar here, Jack!'

Shearing is all over and we've all got our cheques.
Roll up you swag, boys, we're off on the tracks;
The first pub we come to, it's there we'll have a spree,
And everyone that comes along, it's 'Have a drink
    with me!'

Down by the bar the old shearer stands,
Grasping his glass in his thin bony hands;
Fixed is his gaze on a green-painted keg,
Glory, he'll get down on it, ere he stirs a peg.

There we leave him standing, shouting for all hands,
Whilst all around him, every drinker stands;
His eyes are on the cask, which is now lowering fast,
He works hard, he drinks hard, and goes to hell at last!

Traditional

**zack**
  sixpence (in pre-metric currency).

**ziff**
  beard.

**zonk**
  fool.

**zonked**
  rendered paralytic by alcohol, overwork, or both.

# The Great Australian Slanguage

'Tis the everyday Australian
Has a language of his own,
Has a language, or a slanguage,
Which can simply stand alone.
And 'a dicken pitch to kid us'
Is a synonym for 'lie',
And to 'nark it' means to stop it,
And to 'nit it' means to fly!

And a bosom friend's a 'cobber',
And a horse a 'prad' or 'moke',
While a casual acquaintance
Is a 'joker' or a 'bloke',
And his ladylove's his 'donah',
Or his 'clinah' or his 'tart',
Or his 'little bit o' muslin',
As it used to be his 'bart'.

And his naming of the coinage
Is a mystery to some,
With his 'quid' and 'half-a-caser',
And his 'deener' and his 'scrum',
And a 'tin-back' is a party
Who's remarkable for luck,
And his food is called his 'tucker',
Or his 'panem' or his 'chuck'.

A policeman is a 'johnny'
Or a 'copman' or a 'trap',
And a thing obtained on credit
Is invariably a 'strap'.
A conviction's known as 'trouble',
And a gaol is called a 'jug',
And a sharper is a 'spieler'
And a simpleton's a 'tug'.

If he hits a man in fighting
That is what he calls a 'plug',
If he borrows money from you
He will say he 'bit your lug'.
And to 'shake it' is to steal it,
And to 'strike it' is to beg;
And a jest is 'poking borak',
And a jester 'pulls your leg'.

Things are 'cronk' when they go wrongly
In the language of the 'push',
And when things go as he wants 'em
He declares it is 'all cush',
When he's bright he's got a 'napper',
And he's 'ratty' when he's daft,
And when looking for employment
He is 'out of blooming graft'.

*And his clothes he calls his 'clobber'*
*Or his 'togs', but what of that*
*When a 'castor' or a 'kady'*
*Is the name he gives his hat!*
*And our undiluted English*
*Is a fad to which we cling,*
*But the great Australian language*
*Is a truly awful thing!*

W.T. Goodge, 1897

# SLANG-A-SAURUS

Some useful words and phrases, which are listed in alphabetical order in the main section, are grouped in categories in the following pages for quick, easy reference, as a kind of slang thesaurus.

## Alcoholic Delights

amber fluid
chateau de cardboard
coldies
Darwin stubby
deep sinker
gee and tee
grin and chronic
heart-starter
Jimmy Woodser
liquid amber
liquid lunch
lunatic soup
plonk
shearer's joy
stubbies
ten-ounce sandwich
tinnies
tubes
turps
vino

## Angry/Furious

berko
bent as a scrub tick
crooked on
dark on
dirty on
mad as a cut snake
mad as a gumtree
  full of galahs
maggoty
ropeable
toey

## Australia

Bazzaland
Down Under
Oz

## Authentic/Truly
## Australian

all wool and a yard wide
Australian as a meat pie
dinky-di
dinkum
fair dinkum
ridgie-didge
true blue

## Baby/Child

ankle-biter
billy/billy lid

carpet grub
kiddiewink
little Vegemite
nipper
rug-rat
whippersnapper

## *Blowfly*

blowie
butcher's canary

## *Broke/Penniless*

hasn't got a bean
hasn't got a brass razoo
hasn't got a cracker
stony/stony broke
stumped up

## *Broken*

buggered
bung
jiggered
on the blink
onkus
stuffed
up the pole
up the spout
wonky

## *Chat*

bat the breeze
chew the fat

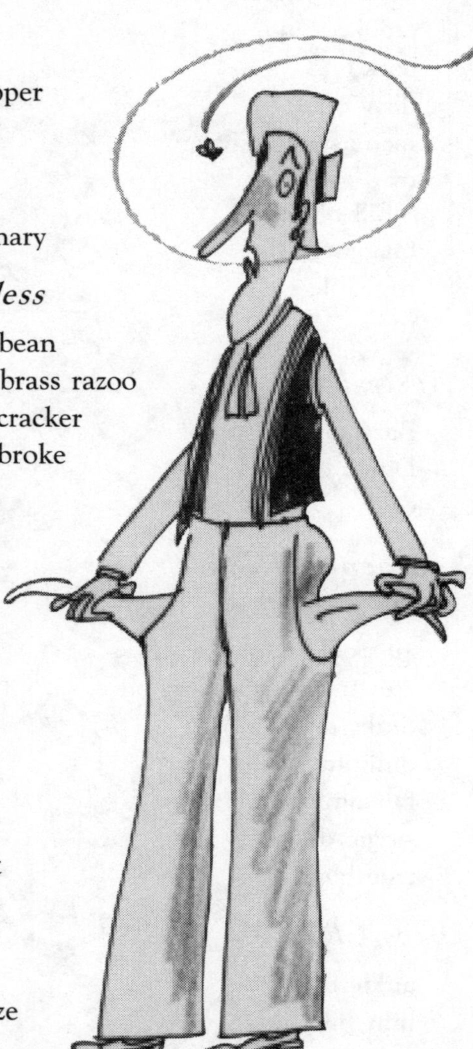

chinwag
yabber

## Country Bumpkin/Rustic Individual

bastard from the bush
bushie/bushwhacker
dubbo
geebung

## Daring

game as a piss-ant
game as Ned Kelly

## Dead

cactus
clagged the bag
dead as mutton chops

## Depressed

happy as bastard on Father's Day
happy as a boxing kangaroo in a fog
miserable as a bandicoot

## Despicable Person

arsehole
dingo
dipstick
low as shark shit
lower than a snake's belly
scumbag
wouldn't piss on him if he was on fire
wouldn't use him for sharkbait

## Difficult

   easy as pushing shit uphill with a toothpick
   easy as spearing an eel with a spoon

## Drunk/Intoxicated

   away with the pixies/birdies
   blind
   dead to the world
   drunk as Chloe
   cut
   elephant's/ elephant's trunk
   flaked out
   full as a boot
   full as a fairy's phone book
   full as a fat woman's sock
   full as a goog
   full as a state school
   full as a tick
   lit up like a Manly ferry
   lit up like a Christmas tree
   loaded
   molly the monk
   out to it
   paralytic
   pissed as a newt
   pissed as a parrot
   pissed as a possum
   rotten/rotten as a chop
   shickered
   shot full of holes
   snakes hissed

stonkered
stunned
tanked
three parts gone
three sheets to the wind
tired and emotional
under the affluence of inkahol
under the weather
well under
zonked

### Eccentric Person

dag
dingbat
poon
ratbag

### Egg

cackleberry
goog/googy
hen fruit

### Excellent

bee's knees
beaut
bobby-dazzler
bonzer
bosker
bottler
crash hot
extra grouse
pure merino

ryebuck
out of the box
trimmer

I'm extremely busy!

### Exhausted

buggered
bushed
clagged out
tuckered out

### Extremely Busy

busy as a one-armed billposter in a gale
flat out like a lizard drinking
flat to the boards
nose down, bum up

### Extremely Cold Weather

brass monkey weather
cold as a bushman's grave
cold enough to freeze the medals off a brass
monkey

### Extremely Hungry

could eat a galah and bark sandwich
could eat a goanna between two slabs of bark
could eat a horse and chase the rider
hungry as a black dog
my stomach thinks me throat's cut

### Extremely Thirsty

dry as a dead dingo's donger
dry as a gum-digger's dog

dry as a kookaburra in the Simpson Desert
dry as a Pom's towel

## Fellow

bleeder
bloke
coot

## Fight/Scuffle

barney
beat the living daylights out of
blue
rough-up
run-in

## Fighting Fit

could kick the arse of an emu
fit as a mallee bull
fit as a mallee trout

## Fired (from Job)

arsed out
got the arse/axe
received the order of the boot

## Flashily Dressed

all laired up
done up like a pet lizard
done up like a pox-doctor's clerk
flash as a rat with a gold tooth
mockered up
pooned up

## Foods

cackleberry (egg)
chook (chicken)
cocky's joy (golden syrup)
damper (bushman's bread)
dead horse (sauce)
dog's eye (meat pie)
floater (meat pie in a bowl of peas or gravy)
fly bog (jam)
goog/goggy-egg (egg)
hen fruit (egg)
johnny cake (type of damper)
murphy (potato)
mystery bags (sausages)
sammie (sandwich)
sanger (sandwich)
sinker (meat pie)
snag (sausage)
underground mutton (rabbit)

## Horse

alligator
brumby
crocodile
moke
prad

## Hotel/Rough Public House

bloodhouse
boozer
lamb-down shop

poison shop
rubbity/rubbity dub

## Idiot

Beecham's Pill
cough drop
dill
dingaling
dingbat
dingdong
dipstick
drongo
droob
dropkick
galah
gink
mopoke
ningnong
nong
wally

## In Trouble

in the cactus
in the poo
on a sticky wicket
up a gumtre
up shit creek without a paddle

## Ineffectual/Incompetent

couldn't fart into a bottle
couldn't fight his way out of a paper bag

couldn't give away cheese at a rats' picnic
couldn't knock the skin off a rice pudding
couldn't last a round in a revolving door
couldn't run a chook raffle in a country pub
couldn't train a choko vine over a country dunny
couldn't win if he started the night before
if he bought a kangaroo it wouldn't hop
must have got his/her licence out of a
  Cornflakes packet
only got one oar in the water
so wet you could shoot ducks off him
sooky
weak as a wet whistle
weak as cats' piss

## Insane/Mentally Deranged

around the twist
barmy as a bandicoot
bats
bent as a scrub tick
bonkers
berko
gone to Gowings
has got some palings off the fence
has got white ants in the woodwork
kangaraoos in the top paddock
mad as a cut snake
mad as a gumtree full of galahs
nits in the network
off your kadoova

## Insults & Invective

'ave a go, ya mug!

bite your bum!

don't pick your nose or your head will cave in!

go and take a running jump at yourself!

go dip your eye in hot cocky cack!

I hope all your chooks turn into emus and knock
  your dunny door down

I wouldn't piss on him if he was on fire

I'll knock your teeth so far down your throat
  you'll have to stick a toothbrush up your arse
  to clean them!

I've seen a better head on a glass of beer

pull your head in!

put a cork/sock in it!

what do you think this is — bush week?

what the bloody hell's crawlin' on you, mate?

you'd make a blowfly sick!

## Items of Clothing

bag of fruit (suit)

bathers (swimming costume)

cossie (swimming costume)

Cunnamulla cartwheel (wide-brimmed hat)

daks (trousers)

duds (trousers)

egg-boiler (bowler hat)

Japanese safety shoes (sandals with thong
  between big toe and next toe)

lunatic hat (wide-brimmed hat)

monkey suit (formal dinner suit)

thongs (sandals with thong between big toe and
next toe)
trunks (swimming costume)

## Kookaburra

breakfast bird
bushman's clock
ha-ha pigeon
jackass
settler's clock
Woop-Woop pigeon

*HA HA HA!*

*Time to get up —*

## Look

Captain Cook
butcher's/butcher's hook
dekko
gander
geek
squiz

## Lonely/Out of Place

all alone like a country dunny
like a lily on a dustbin
like a one-legged man at an arse-kicker's picnic
like a pickpocket at a nudist camp
like a shag on a rock
lonely as a bandicoot on a burnt ridge
on your Pat Malone

## Lout

bodgie
bogan

hoon
larrikin
mug lair
yobbo

## Money

axlegrease
big bickies
dosh
folding stuff
quids
smackers/smackeroos

## New Zealand

Kiwiland
Land of the Long White Shroud
Quaky Isles
Shaky Isles

## Oaths and Exclamations

beauty!
bleeding oath!
buggered if I know!
drop off!
fair crack of the whip!
fair go!
fair suck of the sauce!
good on ya!
Jesus wept!
kiss my arse!
nickywoop!

not on your nelly!
onya!
pull your head in!
put a cork/sock in it!/
put up your dooks!
rattle your daks!
search me!
spitting chips!
strewth!
strike a light!
too right!
tough titty!
turn it up!
up there Cazaly!
you little beauty!
you der!
wouldn't it rip you!
wouldn't it rot your socks!
wouldn't it root you!

## Occupations

*barber*
Sydney Harbour

*bookmaker*
bookie

*boundary rider*
topwire lizard

*carpenter*
chippie

*cattle thief*
duffer
gullyraker

*cattle station worker*
jackaroo, jillaroo

*collector of empty bottles*
bottle-oh

*clergyman*
amen-snorter
Bible-basher
God-botherer
sky pilot

*dairy farmer*
cow-cockie

*dentist*
fang-carpenter
gumpuncher

*dingo-hunter*
dog-stiffener

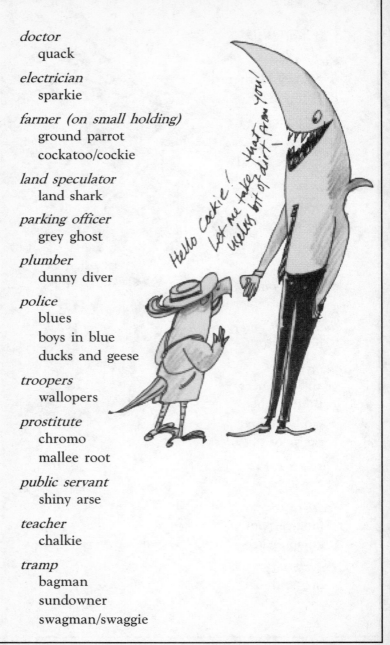

*doctor*
quack

*electrician*
sparkie

*farmer (on small holding)*
ground parrot
cockatoo/cockie

*land speculator*
land shark

*parking officer*
grey ghost

*plumber*
dunny diver

*police*
blues
boys in blue
ducks and geese

*troopers*
wallopers

*prostitute*
chromo
mallee root

*public servant*
shiny arse

*teacher*
chalkie

*tramp*
bagman
sundowner
swagman/swaggie

*Old People*

> crumblies
> old crackers
> oldies

*Pregnant*

> bun in the oven
> in the club
> in the pudding club
> preggers
> up the duff
> up the spout

*Remote Australia*

> back o' Bourke
> Black Stump
> middle of nowhere
> mulga
> Never Never
> outback
> where the crows fly backwards to keep the sun
>   out of their eyes
> woop-woop

*Shark*

    after dark
    Noah/ Noah's ark

*Sheep*

    jumbuck
    yoe

*Sporting Expressions*

    'ave a go, ya mug!
    barrack for
    carn!
    chewie on ya boot!
    crumb-gatherer
    daisy-cutter
    howzat?
    up there Cazaly!

## State Inhabitants

*New South Welshperson*
  cornstalk

*Northern Territorian*
  top-ender

*Queenslander*
  banana-bender

*South Australian*
  crow-eater
  magpie
  pie-eater

*Tasmanian*
  mutton bird
  Tassie tiger

*Victorian*
  cabbage-patcher

*West Australian*
  sandgroper

## Stupid/Slow-witted

brick short of a load
bright as a two-watt bulb
couldn't run guts for a slow butcher
couple of pies short of a grand final
drives uphill with the clutch slippping
few stubbies short of a six-pack
going through life with the porch light on dim
got space to sell between the ears
hasn't got all four paws on the mouse
his/her lift doesn't go all the way to the
 top storey
if his brains were dynamite he couldn't blow his
 hat off
lights are on but there's nobody home
not the full quid
not the full two-bob
nothing between the ears
only fifty cards in the pack
sandwich short of a picnic
short of numbers in the Upper House
snag short of a barbecue
thick as a brick
thick as the dust on a public servant's out-tray
three pots short of a shout
tinny short of a six-pack
wouldn't know his arse from his elbow

## Sycophant

arse-licker
crawler
brown-noser

## Tight-fisted

mean as bird-shit
mean as Hungry Tyson
mingy
so mean that when a fly lands in the sugar he
  shakes it before he kills it
so mean he wouldn't give a rat a railway pie
tight as a bull's arse in fly time
tight as a fish's arse
wouldn't give you the time of day
wouldn't shout in a shark attack

## To Depart

arse off
blow through
choof off
do a flit
do a moonlight flit
do a nickwhoop
nick off
off like a bride's nightie
off like a bucket of prawns
off like a robber's dog
shot shrough like a Bondi tram
skedaddle
went through like a dose of salts
went through without the water bag

## To Die

cark it
croak

do a perish
pass over the Great Divide
see your last gumtree
snuff it

## To Irritate You

get on your goat
give you the irrits
give you the pip
give you the Jimmy Brits
give you the shits

## To Lose Your Temper

blow a fuse
chuck a wobbly
do your block/lolly/nana
flip your lid
get off your bike
get your dander up
go crook
go lemony
go to market
go troppo
spit chips
spit the dummy

## To Urinate

drain the dragon
point Percy at the
    porcelain
splash the boots
strain the potatoes

syphon the python
water the horses

*To Vomit*

bark at the lawn
call 'Ralph'
chunder
drive the porcelain bus
liquid laugh
park a tiger on the rug
speak on the big white telephone
spew
Technicolor yawn
thrown (one's) voice
yodel

## Unlucky Person

if he bought a kangaroo it wouldn't hop
if it was raining palaces he'd be hit on the head
  by a dunny door
if it was raining virgins he'd be locked in the
  dunny with a poofter

## Wife

ball and chain
trouble and strife

## Wild Party

bash
booze-up
rort
shivoo

Can I go to the pub? Darling!

# DIMINUTIVES

Our mania for abbreviating words is one of the first national speech characteristics to strike overseas visitors. Perhaps it is rather infantile, but somehow it adds a kind of cosiness to the world around us. The following are some of our most popular diminutives.

aggro (aggressive)
arvo (afternoon)
Aussie (Australian)
barbie (barbecue)
bickie (biscuit)
blowie (blowfly)
Brissie (Brisbane)
budgie (budgerigar)
cardie (cardigan)
chewie (chewing gum)
Chrissy (Christmas)
ciggie (cigarette)
cockie (cockatoo, cockroach)

coldie (cold beer)
comfy (comfortable)
compo (workers' compensation)
conchie (conscientious objector)
cossie (swimming costume)
cuppa (cup of tea)
deli (delicatessen)
demo (demonstration)
dero (derelict person, vagrant)
footy (football)
garbo (garbage collector)
gladdie (gladiolus)
greeny (conservationist)
hollies (holidays)
hottie (hot water bottle)
intro (introduction)
kindy (kindergarten)
lippie (lipstick)
maggie (magpie)
metho (methylated spirits)
mossie (mosquito)
mushie (mushroom)
myxo (myxomatosis
pokie (poker machine)
postie (postman)
preggers (pregnant)
pressie (present)
rego (car registration)
relly (relative)

sammie (sandwich)
sickie (a day's sick leave)
stubby (small bottle of beer)
sunnies (sunglasses)
swaggie (swagman)
Tassie (Tasmania)
tinnie (beer in a tin)
umpie (umpire)
undies (underpants, underwear)
vegies (vegetables)
wellies (Wellington boots, gumboots)
wino (alcoholic)

# RHYMING SLANG

Our national penchant for rhyming slang is shared by London's Cockneys, and no doubt goes right back to our convict origins. We may have borrowed some commonly-used expressions directly from our English forebears, but many others, such as Dad 'n' Dave and Ned Kelly are true blue Aussie. Some of our most popular examples of rhyming slang are included here.

after dark (shark)
bag of fruit (suit)
Beecham's Pill (dill)
billies/billy lids (kids)
blood and blister (sister)
butcher's/butcher's hook (look)
Captain cook (look)
cat's hiss (piss)
china/china plate (mate)
comic cuts (guts)
country cousin (dozen)
Dad 'n' Dave (shave)
dead horse (sauce)
dog's eye (pie)
ducks and drakes (shakes)
ducks and geese (police)
elephant's/elephant's trunk (drunk)
fairy bower (shower)
Farmer Giles (piles)
frog and toad (road)
Ginger Meggs (legs)
Gregory Peck (cheque)
grin and chronic (gin and tonic)
ham and eggs (legs)
Hawkesbury Rivers (shivers)
hey-diddle-diddle (middle; piddle)
horse's hoof (poof, homosexual man)
Jimmies/Jimmy Brits (shits)
Jimmy Dancer (cancer)
Joe Blake (snake)
Khyber Pass (arse)

Lionel Rose (nose)
mallee root (prostitute)
Mark Foy (boy)
molly/molly the monk (drunk)
mystery bag (snag, sausage)
Ned Kelly (belly)
Noah/Noah's Ark (shark)
on the Murray cod (on the nod)
on your Pat Malone (on your own)
onka/Onkaparinga (finger)
optic nerve (perve)
plates of meat (feet)
plum pud (good)
Sandy McNab (cab)
septic tank (Yank, American)
skin and blister (sister)
squatter's daughter (water)
Steak and Kidney (Sydney)
Sydney Harbour (barber)
total wreck (cheque)
trouble and strife (wife)
Wally Grout (shout)
Williamstown piers (ears)

*I gave that mallee the optic*

NED

# FAUNAL PHRASEOLOGY

Strictly speaking, not all our slang is home-grown. Some of it has become ours through long and frequent use. However, the following phrases, featuring our birds, animals, fish and insects, are definitely a hundred percent dinky di Aussie.

bald as a bandicoot
barmy as a bandicoot
bent as a scrub tick
could eat a galah and bark sandwich
could eat a goanna between two slabs of bark
could kick the arse of an emu
dingo's breakfast
done up like a pet lizard
dry as a dead dingo's donger
dry as a kookaburra's khyber in the
    Simpson Desert
emu's breakfast
fit as a mallee bull
flat out like a lizard drinking
game as a piss-ant
hair like a bush pig's arse
happy as a boxing kangaroo in a fog
haven't they fed the dingoes lately?
high as a dingo's howl
I hope your chooks turn into emus and knock
    your dunny door down
if he bought a kangaroo it wouldn't hop
kangaroos in the top paddock
like a possum up a gumtree
like a shag on a rock
like a stunned mullet
lively as a blowie on a winter's day
lonely as a bandicoot on a burnt ride
lousy as a bandicoot
mad as a gumtree full of galahs
make a proper galah of yourself

miserable as a bandicoot

mouth like the bottom of a cocky's cage

nervous as a mother 'roo in a room full of
  pickpockets.

on the Murray cod

pissed as a parrot

play possum

possum guts

put on a dingo act

racecourse emu

randy as a mallee bull

since Cocky was an egg

stands out like a black crow in a bucket of milk

stirring the possum

stone the crows!

turn dingo

where the crows fly backward
  to keep the dust
  out of their eyes

The Five Mile Press

The Five Mile Press Pty Ltd
950 Stud Road, Rowville
Victoria 3178 Australia
Phone: +61 3 8756 5500
Email: publishing@fivemile.com.au

First published 1999
Reprinted 2000, 2001, 2002, 2003

Editor: Maggie Pinkney
Cartoons: Geoff Hocking
Cover design: Sonia Dixon

Printed in Australia by Griffin Press

National Library of Australia
Cataloguing-in-Publication data
Great Aussie slang
ISBN 1 86463 164 3

1. English language - Australia
- Slang - Dictionaries. I. Pinkney, Maggie
427.994